THE SMART DIVORCE

Proven Strategies and Valuable Advice
from 100 Top Divorce Lawyers, Financial Advisers,
Counselors, and Other Experts

DEBORAH MOSKOVITCH

CHICAGO
REVIEW
PRESS

The information contained in this book is general in nature and does not constitute authoritative legal advice. Laws vary according to state or jurisdiction and may have been amended since publication. This book should only be used in consultation with a licensed lawyer properly familiar with the specific legal matter in question.

For more information, visit the Smart Divorce Web site at www.thesmartdivorce.com.

Library of Congress Cataloging-in-Publication Data

Moskovitch, Deborah.
    The smart divorce : proven strategies and valuable advice from 100 top divorce lawyers, financial advisers, counselors, and other experts / Deborah Moskovitch.
        p. cm.
    Includes bibliographical references and index.
    ISBN-13: 978-1-55652-672-5
    ISBN-10: 1-55652-672-5
    1. Divorce—United States—Handbooks, manuals, etc.   2. Divorce settlements—United States—Popular works.   I. Title.

HQ834.M675 2007
306.89—dc22   2007002287

Cover design: Emily Brackett
Cover image: Chris Andrews/Digital Vision
Interior design: Pamela Juárez

© 2007 by Deborah Moskovitch
All rights reserved
First edition
Published by Chicago Review Press, Incorporated
814 North Franklin Street
Chicago, Illinois 60610
ISBN-13: 978-1-55652-672-5
ISBN-10: 1-55652-672-5
Printed in the United States of America
5 4 3 2 1

To Adam, Elise, and Michael, who provide me with the drive and motivation to be the best parent and role model—and a reason to be.

Contents

Foreword

As a divorce attorney for more than twenty years now, I have certainly seen my fair share of divorces—up close and personal! As a result, I have witnessed the many horrors that can go along with a divorce. So, like many of my colleagues in the field—other family law lawyers, mediators, judges—I am always eager to find ways to make the process of divorce a much smoother transition for those who endure it than it typically is.

I would prefer that my clients be prepared—well armed with tools and techniques that will keep them on the right track throughout the divorce process—than to hear them say afterward that they wished they had known such and such or done so and so. How many times have you heard someone say "I learned so much from my divorce?" I would rather hear people say "I've learned so much *about* my divorce." I want to hear "I know how to select the right lawyer for me, and I know what it is I need to do to organize and control my finances. I've come upon effective ways to parent in the face of divorce and I know precisely how to keep my sanity, even though this life-altering event has the potential to drive me nuts."

In *The Smart Divorce*, Deborah Moskovitch takes the lessons she learned from her divorce and passes them on to others in the same predicament—to make it easier for them. Deborah methodically tackles every phase of the divorce process and offers great wisdom on what to do in the midst of the emotional turmoil and everyday chaos that almost always accompany the incremental stages of divorce. What sets her book apart is that she lays solid groundwork for working toward the future. Through the advice presented on each page, she offers practical stepping stones for "moving on," even before she gets to the chapter that bears that title. She also shares the wisdom of a number of experts who work in the field of divorce, weaving in their points of view—their recommendations—in order to round out her advice.

If you are thinking about divorce, going through one, or still dealing with the aftermath of one, take your time as you read every chapter. Knowledge is power, and it is power that will get you through.

STACY D. PHILLIPS

Stacy D. Phillips is a certified family law specialist licensed by the State Bar of California and the author of the book Divorce: It's All About Control; How to Win the Emotional, Psychological and Legal Wars. *She is the managing partner of Phillips, Lerner, Lauzon & Jamra, a full-service family law firm in Los Angeles, California.*

Acknowledgments

There are a lot of people to whom I am sincerely grateful for their wise counsel and help in getting this book started and finished: Sharon Freedman, my guiding force, mentor, and confidant throughout this process, who believed in me and provided me constant encouragement that I could actually write this book; my agent, Arnold Gosewich, who saw the project's potential and guided me every step of the way; my publisher, Cynthia Sherry, editors Lisa Reardon, Devon Freeny, and Linda Gray, and the team at Chicago Review Press for making my dream a reality and a project that I am proud of; and Dr. Sandy Horodezky and Labe Kagan for planting the seeds of the idea that I should write a book.

I have had so many wonderful people among my panel of readers who have helped shape this book, generously sprinkled it with insights, and ensured the accuracy of information, including Jon Garon, Stacy Phillips, Brenda Christen, Jeffery Wilson, Jim Stoffman, the Honorable W. Ross Foote, Dr. Souhir Benhamida, Mike McCurley, Dr. Larry Fong, Sharon Freedman, Dr. Karen Irvin, Sharon Cohen, Carole Curtis, Debbi Gordon, Lisa Stein, Alan Greenberg, Hal Sclodnick, and Allan Wexler. My appreciation is also directed to Dr. Barbara Jo Fidler and Avra Rosen for the significant amount of time they spent reviewing the manuscript and for their helpful advice, to Carren Oler for her mentoring, support, and thoughts, and to Glenn Lewis for his time and wisdom.

I have many wonderful friends, too numerous to mention, who have propped me up during the rough times, laughed with me during the good times, and been gracious enough to stifle their "I told you so's" as I learned to lead my life in a much smarter way.

I am deeply appreciative of my family, including my parents, Izzy and Sheila Moskovitch; my brother, Stewart Moskovitch; my sister, Sharon Hochman; and their families, whose love and support have been there throughout my divorce, despair, growth, and independence.

And, finally, my heartfelt thanks rests where my heart belongs—with my children, Adam, Elise, and Michael, whose love is always there, no matter how consumed I have been with the writing of this book.

Introduction

The last thing I ever thought I'd do was write a book on divorce. When I was married, I felt that what divorcing families went through was very personal and private. When, after eleven years of marriage, I began to go through the overwhelming process of divorce myself, the idea that I might give anyone practical instruction on how to get through divorce intact would have seemed absurd to me. Every morning I would tell myself, "Today is going to be different." But each day was just another variation of the day before. Carpooling my three young children to programs and school. Making sure they got their hugs and kisses. Racing frantically from work to errands to meetings with my lawyer. Tumbling into bed, exhausted, and waking up a few hours later with any prospects of further sleep drowned out by a symphony of fear, anger, and overwhelming frustration.

Remember the famous T. S. Eliot poem "The Love Song of J. Alfred Prufrock," in which the narrator laments measuring out his life with coffee spoons? I measured out my life with cuts acquired from the piles of paper that were taking over my life. Financial papers. Separation papers. Slips of paper with names I'd scribbled down from newspaper articles about divorce lawyers who had helped their clients "win." A paper trail of emotional letters to my lawyer.

I thought that if I took care of all these papers without spending too much time on their content, I could get through the divorce process faster. But no matter how quickly I turned the pages to keep our lives moving forward, the emotion—and expenses—just kept piling up. When would I finally reach the new chapter of our lives—the one where, as a divorced family, we all lived happily ever after?

I was trying to do everything right. So why wasn't the outcome better? After all, I was a good mother. I had wonderful children and a supportive and lovely cast of family and friends. And hadn't I been responsible by making a relatively quick decision to hire the lawyer I'd set up a meeting with? Wasn't I brave and mature by bottling up my emotions and venting about my divorce only to my lawyer instead of to my friends?

I thought that the way to survive a divorce was to just get through it. I thought I could sidestep the feelings of loss and grief. Wasn't I supposed to just trust my lawyer and the courts to make decisions that were fair? And wasn't I ultimately striving to get myself and my family back on the same path as all the intact families around us? That was the right way to divorce, wasn't it? Wrong. Wrong. Wrong.

It took me seven years to close my divorce file. Most divorces are not this long and drawn out. If I knew then what I know now, I could have shaved a few years off my own divorce journey and saved a significant amount of money. But the experience enriched my own knowledge of divorce, and it inspired me to seek out the very best and brightest divorce lawyers, family therapists, financial advisers, and other experts in North America. Through this book, I'll share with you my own hard-learned lessons, and I'll relay insights and tips from a very special divorce advisory team.

Writing this book has been an incredible journey of understanding. While it was difficult, I have loved every moment of it. I hope this book inspires confidence in you so you can get through this transition. I also want to show you how you can save time, money, and your skin in the process.

Make no mistake. Divorce is hard work. While others around you can provide support and assistance, only you can do the real work to adjust to the reality of your new life so that you and your family can move forward in a healthier, less painful way.

How Is This Book Set Up to Help You?

The Smart Divorce gives you a clear, step-by-step description of the divorce process, from understanding the emotions experienced to choosing a lawyer to considering all the dispute-resolution options to moving through the divorce process to getting on with the rest of your life. Because I've been through a divorce, I am able to: take you from the beginning of the process, when your feelings are raw and exposed; help you understand the need to separate the emotional divorce from the legal divorce; help you understand what it means to develop your divorce strategy; and put you on a more measured, smarter path to getting the divorce itself.

While this book does not offer specific legal advice, it will help you understand what issues the law can and cannot help you resolve, the legal pitfalls to avoid, and the legal and other strategies that can guide you toward resolution. I give you tips on building your own dream divorce team and developing a support network to get you through this difficult time.

Throughout this book are all kinds of practical tips: how to build a short list of the best divorce lawyers in your area; how to hire the right lawyer for you; how to organize your file and cut down on legal costs; and how to understand the healing process you will experience as you go through divorce the smart way.

I also discuss what happens after the divorce is final. The chapters on this topic will help you deal with important matters like coping with your ex, co-parenting your children, moving on, staying in control, and managing your postdivorce life in a healthy way.

As a woman who has weathered a divorce that took me down every possible avenue of the process, I know whereof I write. Whether you are just beginning the divorce process or are in the middle of a bad divorce experience that you would like to turn around, *The Smart Divorce* will enlighten and inspire you on your way to a healthy, happy life.

Meet Your Advisory Team

I am an ordinary woman who, thanks to the extraordinary people who have been part of my journey, learned how to get a smart divorce. Since I got my divorce, and in the process of writing this book, I have talked to over a hundred top-tier divorce lawyers, family therapists, mental health professionals, and financial advisers across North America. The expert strategies of this "advisory team" are woven throughout this book.

Your advisory team will discuss divorce in broad terms to help you avoid tunnel vision about your own situation. The team will assist you in making better-informed emotional, legal, and financial decisions; understanding and assessing your options; choosing your lawyer; strategizing your approach to divorce; staying in control while moving through the process; and avoiding costly mistakes.

Your advisory team also includes some of the most inspiring men and women I've ever met. These individuals, like me, are "experts" from the frontlines of the divorce battles: men and women who have weathered a divorce themselves and come out wiser and sunny side up. I know their stories and smart tips on parenting, dating, relationships, financial considerations, and staying sane are going to help you. Here, then, are your team members.

Lawyers
Sanford K. Ain, Ain & Bank, Washington, D.C.
Thomas G. Bastedo, Bastedo Stewart Smith, Toronto, Ontario
Brenda Christen, Wilson Christen, LLP, Toronto, Ontario

Sharon Cohen, Dickson MacGregor Appell, LLP, Toronto, Ontario

Carole Curtis, Carole Curtis Law Offices, Toronto, Ontario

Daniel Donohue, Law Office of Daniel Donohue, Chicago, Illinois

Philip M. Epstein, QC, Epstein Cole, Toronto, Ontario

Hon. W. Ross Foote (Ret.), Alexandria, Louisiana

Carole S. Gailor, Gailor, Wallis & Hunt, PLLC, Raleigh, North Carolina

Marc Galanter, Professor of Law and South Asian Studies, University of Wisconsin, and LSE Centennial Professor, London School of Economics, Madison, Wisconsin

Dianna Gould-Saltman, Gould-Saltman Law Offices, LLP, Los Angeles, California

Stephen Grant, McCarthy Tétrault, Toronto, Ontario

Geoff Hamilton, Char Hamilton Campbell & Yoshida, Honolulu, Hawaii

Cheryl Lynn Hepfer, Law Offices of Cheryl Lynn Hepfer, Rockville, Maryland

Dena A. Kleeman, Kleeman Kremen Family Lawyers, Beverly Hills, California

Stephen A. Kolodny, Kolodny & Anteau, Beverly Hills, California

Allan R. Koritzinsky, Foley & Lardner, LLP, Madison, Wisconsin

Armin Kuder, Kuder, Smoller & Friedman, Washington, D.C.

Nicholas A. Leto Jr., Veltmann & Leto, LLP, San Diego, California

Glenn C. Lewis, Lewis Law Firm, Washington, D.C.

James Colin MacDonald, QC, MacDonald & Partners, Toronto, Ontario

Madam Justice June Maresca, Ontario Court of Justice, Brampton, Ontario

Mike McCurley, McCurley Orsinger McCurley Nelson &
Downing, LLP, Dallas, Texas

Jill L. McLeod, Jill L. McLeod, Lawyer and Mediator, Toronto,
Ontario

Steven A. Mindel, Feinberg, Mindel, Brandt, Klein & Kline,
LLP, Los Angeles, California

Craig Neville, Watson Goepel Maledy, LLP, Vancouver, British
Columbia

Harold Niman, Niman Zemans Gelgoot, Toronto, Ontario

Carren S. Oler, Law Office of Carren S. Oler, Rockville,
Maryland

Joan Patsy Ostroy, Law and Mediation Offices of Joan Patsy
Ostroy, Los Angeles, California

Connolly Oyler, Oyler & Woldman, Santa Monica, California

Mark S. Patt, Trope and Trope, Los Angeles, California

Paul Pellman, Paul S. Pellman, Barrister at Law, Toronto,
Ontario

Stacy D. Phillips, Phillips, Lerner, Lauzon & Jamra, Los Angeles, California

Avra Rosen, Law Offices of Avra Rosen, Toronto, Ontario

Jack A. Rounick, Flamm, Boroff & Bacine, PC, Blue Bell,
Pennsylvania

Patrick D. Schmidt, Thomson, Rogers, Toronto, Ontario

J. Lindsey Short, Short Jenkins Kamin, LLP, Houston, Texas

Judith E. Siegel-Baum, Wolf, Block, Schorr and Solis-Cohen,
LLP, New York, New York

Jim Stoffman, Taylor McCaffrey, Winnipeg, Manitoba

Ronald Supancic, Family Law Offices of Ronald M. Supancic,
Woodland Hills, California

Nicole Tellier, Nicole Tellier Law Offices, Toronto, Ontario

Fern Topas Salka, Fern Topas Salka, Los Angeles, California

Marshall W. Waller, Feinberg & Waller, Calabasas and Beverly
Hills, California

Peter M. Walzer, Walzer & Melcher, LLP, Beverly Hills, California

Stuart Webb, Stuart Webb Collaborative Lawyer, Minneapolis, Minnesota

Mary H. Wechsler, Wechsler Becker, LLP, Seattle, Washington

Paige Leslie Wickland, Fancher & Wickland, San Francisco, California

David M. Wildstein, Wilentz, Goldman & Spitzer, PA, Woodbridge, New Jersey

Jeffery Wilson, Wilson Christen, LLP, Toronto, Ontario

Edward L. Winer, Moss & Barnett, Minneapolis, Minnesota

Lorne Wolfson, Torkin Manes, Toronto, Ontario

Nancy Zalusky Berg, Walling Berg & Debele, PA, Minneapolis, Minnesota

Mediators

Kenneth Cloke, Center for Dispute Resolution, Santa Monica, California

William A. Eddy, National Conflict Resolution Center, San Diego, California

Dr. Larry Fong, Fong Mediate, Calgary, Alberta

Lenard Marlow, Divorce Mediation Professionals, New York, New York

Carl D. Schneider, PhD, Mediation Matters, Bethesda, Maryland

Mental Health, Social Work, and Adult and Family Professionals

Dr. Dan Baker, Life Enhancement Program at Canyon Ranch, Tucson, Arizona

Dr. Souhir Benhamida, Seattle, Washington

Dr. G. Andrew H. Benjamin, University of Washington, Seattle, Washington

Dr. Gary Chase, Santa Monica, California

Dr. Nancy Cohen, Toronto, Ontario

Elaine Cole, Sherman Oaks, Culver City, California

Dr. Bruce Copeland, Bethesda, Maryland

Tina R. Crowe, Marina del Rey, California

Dr. Bruce Derman, Woodland Hills, California

Melisse Eidman, San Ramon, California

Dr. Robert E. Emery, Center for Children, Families, and the Law, University of Virginia, Charlottesville, Virginia

Dr. Sheila Rodger Faucher, Toronto, Ontario

Dr. Barbara Jo Fidler, Toronto, Ontario

Elinor Gertner, Jewish Family and Child Service, Toronto, Ontario

Dr. George Glass, Houston, Texas

Dr. Sol Goldstein, Toronto, Ontario

Dr. Jonathan W. Gould, Charlotte, North Carolina

Dr. Mark Goulston, Los Angeles, California

Dr. Wendy Hutchins-Cook, Seattle, Washington

Dr. Karen Irvin, St. Paul, Minnesota

Dr. Howard H. Irving, Toronto, Ontario

David Kuroda, Torrance, California

Renee Leff, JD, Board Certified Diplomate Fellow in Forensic Science, Encino, California

Dr. Jayne A. Major, Breakthrough Parenting Services, Inc., Los Angeles, California

Mindy Mitnick, Minneapolis, Minnesota

Diane Moody, McWhinney Metcalfe and Associates, Toronto, Ontario

Dr. Raymond Morris, Toronto, Ontario

Dr. Joan Pinkus, Vancouver, British Columbia

Dr. Terri Romanoff-Newman, Minneapolis, Minnesota

Dr. Benjamin M. Schutz, Springfield, Virginia

Dr. Michael J. Spierer, Madison, Wisconsin

Dr. Philip M. Stahl, Gilbert, Arizona

Dr. Patricia Sullivan, San Francisco, California

Dr. Peggy Thompson, Family Psychological Services, Orinda,
   California
Dr. Ken Waldron, Waldron Kriss and Associates, Madison,
   Wisconsin
Dr. Richard A. Warshak, Dallas, Texas

Financial Experts

Linda Brent, Brent Valuations, Inc., Toronto, Ontario
Farley Cohen, Navigant Consulting, Toronto, Ontario
Andrew Freedman, Cole & Partners, Toronto, Ontario
Beverly Hanna, Vancouver Financial Planning Consultants, Inc.,
   Vancouver, British Columbia
Thomas Harjes, CPA, Virchow, Krause & Company, LLP,
   Minneapolis, Minnesota
Michael Penner, Marmer Penner, Inc., Toronto, Ontario
Carol Ann Wilson, Carol Ann Wilson, LLC, Boulder, Colorado

Those Who Have Been There

Over the last ten years I've spoken with incredible men, women,
and children who've provided firsthand accounts of the divorce
experience. They have contributed significantly to my insights and
wisdom about divorce—they in fact have influenced the way I've
lived my life, which is to have moved forward in a healthy, positive
way. I thank them for their help. But in the interest of their privacy
they shall remain anonymous.

1

Understanding Divorce

di·vorce (dĭ-vôrs', -vōrs') *n. the legal dissolution of a marriage; v. to sever the marital relationship with a spouse by a judgment or decree of divorce.*

If divorce were as straightforward as the dictionary definition, the process would be a whole lot easier. Couples, children, and extended families could carry on with their lives as if nothing much had changed. The "legal dissolution" could involve collegial discussions in lawyers' boardrooms followed by the signing of papers, a handshake, and best wishes all around. Actually, some lawyers and judges favor the dictionary definition. "Treat your divorce as a business transaction," they urge couples who come to see them. There's a lot of wisdom in this piece of advice, if it is applied to the legal side of divorce. But this view neglects the emotional side of divorce. It's as if they're saying, "Business partnerships . . . marriage partnerships . . . what's the difference?"

Most people who have gone through a divorce—and most lawyers and judges, too—will tell you that the dictionary definition captures only one small part of the reality of divorce. Divorce is an extremely demanding and painful experience riddled with complications. When divorce isn't tragic, it's at least extremely disappointing. A relationship that was launched in a hopeful wedding ceremony followed by candlelight and the celebratory clinking of glasses has turned into a fire fueled by fear, anger, grief, and guilt.

I know, having gone through divorce myself, that it is both a business transaction (which I certainly didn't realize at the time) and a time of deep emotional distress (which I experienced all too well). And while it would be really nice if the two elements could be handled one after the other—you could spend a few years dealing with the emotional issues, and then, heart and head clear, go through the legal process—I also know that emotions and legal processes cannot be clinically separated.

Every divorce involves three intertwined components: financial, emotional, and legal. The traditional judicial system is equipped to handle only the legal aspect, and it often ignores or exacerbates the remaining two. Some lawyers settle almost every case early, and others settle after much emotional trauma and expense; however, most settlements are couched in purely legal terms, offering little help or understanding of how to live with the other two elements.

Hon. W. Ross Foote (Ret.), Alexandria, Louisiana

But the ultimate challenge of divorce is precisely this: the legal issues come up at the beginning of the process, when you're least able to deal with them objectively. At this stage, even if you're relieved to be separated from your spouse, you're still going to be off-kilter. Virtually no one walks away from a marriage with a slight mopping of the brow and the casual remark "Well, I'm glad that's over with."

What Is a Smart Divorce?

What, then, is a smart divorce? A smart divorce is one in which you accept that:

- both the emotional and legal sides of divorce are real and valid
- you have to go through both, and pretty much at the same time
- emotions and the legal process cannot be perfectly sealed off from each other

With a smart divorce, however, you also realize that the pain of divorce can be lessened dramatically by properly handling the competing emotional and legal sides of divorce. The smart approach to divorce:

- affirms the emotions experienced in marital breakups
- helps you gain perspective on your legal options early on
- assists you in making informed decisions, protected from the damage that uncontrolled emotions can cause
- guides you in meeting your children's best interests
- moves you and your spouse back into single status, ready to get on with the rest of your lives while fulfilling the responsibilities that flow from your former married state

Why is it critical that you get a smart divorce? Because you—and your children, if you have any—are going to be living the rest of your lives with the results of the decisions you make during the divorce process. You want to make decisions that will allow all of you to live without regret.

A smart divorce is one where the parties and counsel remain civil during the process. The schedule for the children is worked out reasonably peacefully, and the parties seem to be able to co-parent reasonably well. The monetary results are fair to both parties—no one is getting a financial killing one way or the other. A careful, competent judgment is written, spelling out the terms of settlement, so as to assure the settlement "sticks"—the parties are not going to return to court later to try and set the settlement aside.

Lawyer Dena A. Kleeman, Kleeman Kremen
Family Lawyers, Beverly Hills, California

To get a smart divorce, you have to understand how to keep the "two divorces"—the emotional divorce and the legal divorce—as separate as possible. The members of this book's advisory team of divorce lawyers, therapists, and marriage experts are unanimous in saying that emotions should be kept out of the legal proceedings as much as possible. Letting your emotions become part of your legal decision-making process will ratchet up your legal costs, cause you to make faulty decisions, prolong the divorce process, and hold everyone back—yourself included—from moving on to a rosier future. So let's take a closer look at these two sides of divorce.

The Emotional Divorce

I had been crying myself to sleep every night for a good long time. But after ten months of marriage counseling and therapy, and much waffling, I finally realized that the only solution was for my husband and me to live "separately and apart."

I thought I had it figured out. I thought that when I finally came to terms with my marriage being over, the divorce would follow in an adult fashion. After all, we were husband and wife and parents. Surely things couldn't be so bad. We parented together; why couldn't we parent apart? But then strong, if not irrational, emotions from both sides got in the way. Sometimes it got so heated that I wasn't sure what we were fighting over. Was it finances? Was it the children's best interests? Was it trying to regain control over our own lives? The lines became blurred.

What I thought would be relatively straightforward and painless became complex and painful. I was shocked to see the smart, sensible me succumbing to unclear thinking. The divorce process was taking over my life, and my legal bills were mounting—and I was just getting started! I know now that I was firmly in the grip of many of the dynamics that are part of the emotional divorce.

The Shame and Blame Game

I felt like a victim. I was a victim. I had been wronged, and I couldn't let go of this thought. I wanted fairness. I wanted justice. How could this have happened to me, a good wife and mother? How could I hold my head up around my friends, most of whom were married with children and seemed to be doing just fine? I felt like such an outsider, no longer knowing where I fit in, especially any time I had to say, "No, actually, my husband and I have separated."

Blame not only rhymes with shame; it's the automatic response to it. You feel exposed. To divert attention from yourself, you lash out, blaming your spouse. It's very tempting at this point to look to the law as something that can help you show everyone who's really to blame.

The Desire for Revenge

Once the separation and divorce processes get rolling, many divorcing people's knee-jerk reaction is to seek revenge. They may have been leading separate lives together—an extremely sad, lonely, and frustrating way to live. And now they feel exposed: their private problems as a couple have become public knowledge—perhaps even juicy morsels of speculation and gossip. They are hurt, angry, and raw. And, whether only one partner is pushing for divorce or both are on the same page, the anger can spark the feeling: *someone's going to pay for getting me into this mess.*

There is no revenge in divorce; there are only legal bills.

Lawyer Steven A. Mindel, Feinberg, Mindel, Brandt,

Klein & Kline, LLP, Los Angeles, California

Revenge can take many forms. A common one, unfortunately, is using the kids to get back at each other. Parental childishness over visiting times, purchases, school trips, and so on can turn kids into weapons skillfully deployed by Mom and Dad. Some parents even try to enlist their children on their side of the battle.

If I had a nickel for every time someone came into my office and said, "I'd rather pay you than pay my spouse," I'd be rich. My response to that is to say, "That's moronic. Save your money. At least keep it in your family. Use it to pay child support instead."

Lawyer Brenda Christen, Wilson Christen, LLP, Toronto, Ontario

---

Some divorcing couples seek revenge by lashing out at each other's families. Couples may have had perfectly warm relationships with in-laws, but now a line is drawn in the sand, with the camps forming up, usually along family lines.

I deliver my elevator speech to clients who are seeking vengeance. I tell them, "Call me when you hate wasting money more than you hate your soon-to-be ex."

Lawyer Steven A. Mindel, Feinberg, Mindel, Brandt,

Klein & Kline, LLP, Los Angeles, California

If this aspect of the emotional divorce is allowed to mix with the legal decisions you have to make, you may find yourself hiring the type of lawyer known for fighting to win at any cost. Well, not any cost: your cost. You may add weeks, months, and even years of suffering and expense by using the law to exact as much emotional and financial pain on your spouse as possible or by looking for an elusive sense of justice rather than getting yourself into a new life.

What makes the process adversarial is deception, posturing, unreasonable demands, expectations that there will be some kind of restorative justice, which courts are not quick to fully address. Lost hopes and dreams. That's not compensable in the way that the loss is experienced.

Lawyer Carren S. Oler, Law Office of Carren S. Oler, Rockville, Maryland

---

One of the most difficult things for patients to accept, say therapists, is that they will never get the vindication or apology that they want so badly or feel they deserve.

Divorcing people hurt so much that they want to unload the hurt on each other. They go looking for the meanest, baddest lawyer in town. They strike out at each other because they're in the pain of being rejected, and they fear they will never find anyone else to love. They fear that they will be living a lesser life. I advise, "Let's think about the consequences. Do we really want to stay in litigation for two years? What about the children?" There's enough heartbreak here. Let's not add to it.

Psychologist Dr. Dan Baker, Director, Life Enhancement Program at Canyon Ranch, Tucson, Arizona

The Disruption of Routines

At first, separation may seem pretty natural. What's so different? From your perspective, you are relieved not to be involved in daily battles. You welcome the emotional space you now have. From the children's perspective, it can seem as if the absent parent is away on a trip. In fact, while they may see one parent less often, he or she may be more attentive to them as a visitor than he or she was as an in-house parent. Some therapists call such a person "the born-again parent." (I'll return to this aspect of divorce in chapter 8.)

I quickly learned that life is more complex than that. School concerts and athletic events, visits to grandparents and uncles and aunts, birthday parties, weekend outings—anything that meant anything to our family—was drastically different. Where everything happened so naturally before, now I had to think about where I should sit, how I should react, how I should—or even if I should—communicate. Traditions big and small were changing, too. Our routines and the delightful planned exceptions to routines—vacations, family outings on the weekend, dinners at our favorite restaurants—most of these were compromised by the big change in our lives.

Adults can introduce stability to their own and their children's lives pretty quickly, but most adults cannot shake the feeling of guilt—guilt over upsetting their children and the larger family.

Changes to Your Social Life

I felt awkward when I turned up at social events unescorted. I would laugh and pretend to be happy. But when people asked me about life and work, I could sum up a whole year in five minutes. If I threw in the details of my divorce, well, that could have lasted five hours. But that would have been a good way to isolate myself even further: very few people want to discuss divorce at a party. I knew I was a good mother, a person with lots of interests, a loyal friend. But I felt different, rattling around in society with nothing to ground me in the events I was a part of.

Just as family members align themselves with the spouse they are related to, friends of a couple also begin to choose sides. When, because of your kids, you go to events where friends from both sides are present—well, it can seem like the start of a whole new Cold War. Sometimes, though, it isn't about how people feel about you; it's your situation they have a hard time accepting.

Do you know how tempting it is to avoid people who are going through a terrible illness or who have just lost a loved one? The whole thing makes you feel uneasy. You don't know what to say. Well, people treated me and my husband the same way. Some of our best friends avoided both of us like the plague. I suspect that some of them didn't want to face the precariousness of their own relationships.

I think the worst feeling I had, especially at the beginning, was that I was losing my identity. I was being sucked into an emotional vortex, with everything changing around me. I wasn't sure who I was anymore. That's not a surprise when you consider that my whole world had been based on couples: couples who were friends of ours from our school days or work; couples whom we'd met socially; couples who were the parents of our children's friends. It's a Noah's Ark society; with everyone around me going about two by two, where did I fit in on the boat?

Dealing with the Emotional Divorce

Although the issues laid out above just scratch the surface of the emotional divorce, all of them are normal and to be expected. But you can see, I hope, that you are in danger of making the wrong legal and financial decisions at this point unless you compartmentalize these emotions.

What happens when anger and emotions are involved is that people do not see things clearly. For instance, the wife is so mad that she's not thinking about how she should divide the property equally and what's a fair value to put on the house and how the children should be shared. She's just mad and wants to get at the husband. Then she uses the lawyer as a tool to carry out her anger, without regard to the cost and what she and her spouse are doing to their children. It's usually a case of good people acting badly, and they can't see it.

Lawyer, Nicholas A. Leto Jr., Veltmann & Leto, LLP, San Diego, California

You really need to take the time to process your thoughts and consider the likely outcome of your actions. It probably sounds impossible to you, but it can be done.

The emotional component of divorce is like a five-hundred-pound gorilla. It's there, and it sometimes causes people to do stuff. I tell people that I could have their judgment prepared by the next day. It's just a document, and I could predict in most cases what is going to happen two years from now. But because of the emotions, because of the fear, the anger, the confusion, and the sadness, it takes a long time for them to get through the process.

Lawyer Peter M. Walzer, Walzer & Melcher, LLP, Beverly Hills, California

So how should you deal with the emotional divorce? And how can you keep it separate from the legal divorce?

The legal divorce, as we will see later in this chapter and throughout this book, is all about laws, strategies, moves, and countermoves. It is not necessarily about what we feel is right, or best, or just.

I argue that our object as lawyers or mediators should be to solve a problem—namely, how each of you is going to manage in the future and the obligation that each of you should have to the other based upon the circumstances of your marriage. But, though laws were created to solve that problem, the procedures that the law created are not very good ones. Following legal rules won't leave you with justice, and what happens is that we lose sight of the problem and become absorbed with the process.

Mediator and lawyer Lenard Marlow,
Divorce Mediation Professionals, New York, New York

In civil cases, courts determine the duties of the parties, some liability for breaching those duties, and the dollar amount to be paid to compensate—partially or fully—for that breach. There is no justice to be sought, just an identification of the duties, liabilities, and amounts due. Courts are powerless to provide anything approaching justice.

Even so, we can't turn on a switch and become robots when we enter lawyers' offices or the family law courtroom. Emotions and passions are almost always involved in the legal process. For instance, if someone has been defamed, he is going to feel passionate about using the legal system to clear his name. If someone has been wrongfully fired, she is going to want the legal system to make it clear that she is a responsible professional who was let go unfairly. The same is true in divorce.

Divorce is one of the most emotional experiences a person will ever face. The negative emotions associated with it are responsible for more than hurt feelings; they affect the final outcome of settlement negotiations. If children are involved, they will suffer. It is in your best interests to approach divorce from an amicable perspective. This will allow you to put on your business hat, which is critical for reaching a successful settlement. It will also allow you to put on your effective parent hat, which is critical for helping you get your children through this difficult process.

Lawyer Nancy Zalusky Berg, Walling Berg &
Debele, PA, Minneapolis, Minnesota

The key, though, is to let your passions fuel the legal process while not letting them foul up the legal process. You're going to need the energy of your emotions and desire for justice to get you through the divorce. However, you do not want these feelings to push you into foolish decisions, prolonging the agony and upping the bill.

There is no justice in the courts, even for people who do have common sense and realistic expectations. It's a system of subjective human beings, not a justice system.

Lawyer Peter M. Walzer, Walzer & Melcher, LLP, Beverly Hills, California

Imagine yourself, then, owning your emotions and dealing with them by talking to wise friends or therapists so that the anguish is drawn off. This will enable you to make legal decisions more rationally. And imagine that you have yourself in the proper frame of mind, seeing divorce as a job, basically, that you have to do in order to move on to a better life for you and your loved ones. Your emotions are there to give you the energy and stamina you need, but you are not going to allow them to influence your decisions negatively.

The Legal Divorce

How Does the Divorce Process Begin and Progress?

Couples must live separately and apart before divorce will be endorsed by a judge. The divorce process usually begins when your or your spouse's lawyer files an application to divorce. It means that the separation is permanent and that there is no chance of reconciliation. This letter from the lawyer starts the negotiation process. In most jurisdictions, there is *no-fault divorce*, meaning that from a legal and business point of view, the reasons behind the divorce—how the divorcing spouses behaved while they were living together—are generally not relevant.

In a no-fault divorce, conduct during marriage doesn't matter. So, say a husband wants out, say he's had many affairs; that doesn't count. And when the time comes to divide up the property, his wife may feel screwed by the system, because the system is not recognizing, to her mind, an obviously derelict spouse. The law doesn't accommodate that. The law says fifty-fifty division.

Lawyer Geoff Hamilton, Char Hamilton
Campbell & Yoshida, Honolulu, Hawaii

The legal bottom line is that divorce dissolves a marriage through a legal transaction with accompanying financial arrangements. These arrangements are determined by analyzing the couple's financial documents to figure out their assets and liabilities. In most cases, the assets are eventually divided according to what the law deems fair, providing each party with a portion of the economic pie. The best interests of any children are placed first and foremost to determine their living arrangements and each parent's childcare responsibilities. Child support and spousal support, if required, are determined. All this is based on the premise of what is reasonable.

Whatever form of dispute resolution the couple uses (the options are discussed at length in chapter 4), the end result is a divorce decree. This is submitted for the courts to review and is signed by the judge, and then the marriage is over. I remember when, one day, opening my mail, there in my hands was this piece of paper—a document that was signed and sealed by the judge. I was now divorced. A single woman, a single parent. It was kind of surreal. There was no ceremony or celebration indicating the end, as there had been when the marriage began.

What the Law Can and Can't Do

There are many issues that just do not fit inside the legal arena. Your lawyer's job is to listen to what you, the client, want, and to secure the best outcome for you. Based on the information that you provide, your lawyer can make a settlement proposal to your spouse's lawyer, prepare a petition for dissolution of marriage, prepare a separation agreement, draft a consensual judgment finalizing the outstanding issues between you and your spouse, and have a judge sign it. But your lawyer can't make your spouse change. He or she can't change the law that dictates whether you are going to have to pay your spouse for a portion of the value of your business, or whether you are going to have to pay child support.

The law cannot make you happy. The law cannot make your spouse a better mother or father. What the law can do is switch money from one pocket to another and make orders, which people will or won't follow.

Justice is sort of an amorphous concept that, frankly, doesn't necessarily happen in a courthouse.

Lawyer Dianna Gould-Saltman, Gould-Saltman
Law Offices, LLP, Los Angeles, California

I knew a judge who once, when he was about to render his decision, told the divorcing couple, "I hope you did not come to court this morning expecting me to give you anything. I have nothing to give you. Whatever you came to court with, you will leave with less. You will be better served going back out to the hallway and reaching a settlement on your own."

Lawyer Ronald Supancic, Family Law Offices of Ronald M. Supancic,
Woodland Hills, California

What's Next for You?

I hope that at this point you are beginning to understand the necessity of compartmentalizing the emotional divorce and the legal divorce. I hope that you are becoming realistic about what the law can and cannot do. But at the end of the day, what should your goal be?

All of the professionals I consulted, in every field, say the same thing: you should take the opportunity to experience personal growth and gain insight, and work toward a better life than the one you are now living. Yes, it's true that this is more easily said than done. But this is the attitude that will help you navigate the legal process and ensure a better future.

The best that can be expected during the divorce process is that both sides will accept their responsibilities, accept the fact that their marriage didn't work out, and agree that neither is a bad person because of it. Ideally, no one will fling much criticism, and the couple will work through the process in a way that allows both of them to keep their heads up high and believe that they weren't dragged through the mud.

What makes for a smart divorce is the recognition that you have to move on. The financial parts of family law are not very complicated. An accountant sorts through all that and makes it clear. What separates those who can obtain a smart divorce from those who can't is this quality of being prepared to move on. They've done their mourning, to the extent that mourning is involved. And they have come to recognize that they're not victims. "This is what life has to offer. So let's move on." This helps you see the problems differently.

Lawyer Jeffery Wilson, Wilson Christen, LLP, Toronto, Ontario

Fortunately, the couple won't be alone in their efforts. Task forces, think tanks, divorce roundtables, and organizations are searching for ways to help people divorce with dignity and preserve relationships, and to come up with a less acrimonious process of separation. The rights and responsibilities that people have throughout divorce have changed dramatically in recent years. The laws have changed, and so too have many lawyers.

There is a paradigm shift in thinking that has affected the more senior lawyers. Everybody was a hawk; now everybody is a dove. They're doves in the sense that they see the larger picture, and recognize that people need to get on with their lives. They work out something that they can recommend to their client as being fair, appropriate, and consistent with the law—something that will allow the client to get on with it.

Lawyer Stephen Grant, McCarthy Tétrault, Toronto, Ontario

But it's still up to you to establish realistic goals and expectations in order to pave the way for a smart divorce. Of course, that isn't possible when you're despairing of ever getting out of the emotional hole you find yourself in. The next chapter will discuss how to come to grips with your emotions and take care of yourself during this turbulent time.

2

Staying Sane
Throughout Divorce

As I was divorcing, I went through a kaleidoscope of intense feelings: fear, anger, rage, sadness, guilt, shock, frustration, and relief. I wanted desperately to piece my world back together, but I didn't want to feel the emotions or even to face what had happened in my marriage. My grief and fear manifested itself in anxiety and physical aches and pains.

Day after day, week after week, I waited impatiently—and passively—for my fate to be altered. All I wanted was to feel happy again. When not enough happened, I sank deeper into helplessness, blaming myself for the pain that my children and I were feeling. The more helpless I felt, the more I resorted to the shame and blame game and played a victim.

It seemed that no one understood what I was going through. It is a mystery to me how the English language can confine the word "sad" to a mere three letters. In the first year of divorcing, I was so sad that my emotions felt like a country I had to walk through all alone. What made me feel lonelier still was that everyone felt they had the right to comment on what I was going through. Much unsolicited advice was given—advice that, although well intentioned, was absurd and inappropriate. I felt that friends and family didn't really understand what I was going through. How could they? I didn't understand myself.

What You May Be Feeling—and What to Do About It

Divorce has become so common today that people underestimate how powerful an experience it truly is. People don't know how to react to divorcing people. When one loses a spouse through death, it is expected that there will be a mourning period, and people are respectful; whereas during divorce, people say things like "You're better off without him," "I never liked her in the first place," and on and on. These types of comments don't make things better and can actually make you feel worse. If they only knew all the emotions you were going through, they might not be so flippant.

Grief

Grief is not a mental disorder; it is a natural, if painful, emotion that must be worked through. Throughout my divorce, though, I would at times get stuck in my grief and feel paralyzed. I would vent and cry about the same issues over and over again. It certainly was not productive. Finally, my good friend said to me (a year after my separation), "You're very difficult to be around these days." I guess I'd been releasing a lot of negative energy. No matter how supportive your friends and family are, they will get tired of hearing the same story over and over. If you're still telling that same story a year later, you're stuck. Feelings of sadness are part of a natural grieving process, but you must deal with them in order to move on.

Grief presents an opportunity to make important choices and think about the life you want to lead. There is an incredible amount of emotional work and healing that needs to be done when you're grieving, especially during the first year or two of going through divorce.

Emotional healing is hugely important, and the idea of grieving is always there in divorce. It gets to a more basic strategy for dealing with anger, and that is that anger is an easy emotion; it's easy to be mad. It's a safe emotion, too. But what you need to do is recognize how you are feeling, then look beneath that feeling. And beneath the anger, oftentimes there is grief. Other times there is longing; other times there are fear and anxiety.

Professor of Psychology Dr. Robert E. Emery, Director, Center for Children, Families, and the Law, University of Virginia, Charlottesville, Virginia

---

What's the Grief About?

Why was I grieving? I was grieving over the unknowns ahead: How would divorce affect our children? What would people around me think, and how would they react to me and our kids? What was life going to be like as a single parent? I was also grieving over all the turmoil—a slow-moving legal process, delays caused by the other side, and adjourned court hearings. These are all common causes of grief during a divorce, and you may experience them yourself.

Another cause of grief is the fact that you are experiencing losses that you probably never thought would happen: The death of your marriage. The loss of your identity as a couple. The loss of a life you shared. The loss of having your children with you day in and day out. The loss of your family as you knew it, and of your spouse's family, and of the whole extended family. The loss of your social life as a couple. The loss of status or friends. The loss of a partner to talk to about the little events of your day to and to share household responsibilities with. The loss of someone sitting in the passenger seat of the car, someone to make plans with—all of the day-to-day sharing that gets taken for granted.

What makes divorce so overwhelming is that it affects what therapists call your "world view": your sense of identity, safety, and security, your beliefs about other people, and your understanding of the kind of place the world is to live in. This is traumatic; almost everything you thought you knew about yourself, the world, and your place in it can be rocked to the core. It's a whole package of beliefs that is completely wiped out when the marriage ends.

What Does the Grief Look Like?

Mourning the loss of a marriage is similar to mourning the loss of a loved one through death, with a significant difference. You don't necessarily have the closure that comes with losing a loved one. If you share children, then this person, whether you like it or not, is still in your life and is a constant reminder of the loss. In dealing with the death of a loved one, the healing process is a slow but steady upward incline toward better days. With divorce, it's more like climbing the Rocky Mountains, with many peaks and valleys of emotion and many bumps along the way. You begin to move forward, but then the holidays arrive and you fall back as you find yourself alone or no longer included in annual traditions. A new relationship moves you forward, but if you lose that relationship, it becomes another setback. If the legal side of divorce becomes overly stressful, you're set back even further. The road to recovery is a jagged line that goes up and down because, as you try to get better emotionally, these experiences seem to get in the way.

The two divorcing people rarely experience the stages of grieving at exactly the same time. It takes two to marry, but only one to divorce. Many times, the decision to separate is made primarily by one person, blindsiding the person who was left. By the time the decision to leave the marriage has finally been communicated, the decision maker may have already grieved the loss of the marriage and be ready to move forward, while the one who is left is in shock, and is years behind the other on the road to recovery. So you've got a divorcing couple who are in different emotional states. One person is thinking, "Let's get this over with," and the other is saying, "Whoa, I need to slow down, digest, and regroup." Grieving during divorce is done individually, not as a couple. While you may think your spouse should be more concerned about how you are feeling, or vice versa, it's everyone for themselves. That can make the transition even more difficult. Not only are you forced to apply rational thought and reason at a time when you can't think straight, but you've quite possibly lost the concern and support of the person you trusted most.

Grieving is a three-part process, with each phase having its own intense period of mourning. Each phase occurs in waves—highs and lows—and then gradually tapers off.

1. **Love.** The opposite of love is indifference. What you want to feel is a diminishing love. If you hate that person, it is still emotionally draining and time consuming.
2. **Anger.** Feelings of revenge, of wanting your spouse to pay for this decision.
3. **Sadness.** You find yourself thinking, "What am I going to do?"

You will cycle back and forth through these stages. You are grieving alone—you don't have a partner to *grieve* with—and you are each grieving different losses. This causes you to wonder: *Why doesn't he/she understand? Why is he/she so cold? Why is he/she so irrational?*
Professor of Psychology Dr. Robert E. Emery, Director, Center for Children, Families, and the Law, University of Virginia, Charlottesville, Virginia

---

How You'll Get Through the Grief

Research indicates that it can take people anywhere from two to five years to adjust to divorce. One thing that helped me immediately was when I realized that I was not alone. I remember feeling that a weight had actually been lifted from my shoulders when my therapist told me that just about everybody feels vulnerable, alone, and unprepared for divorce. Having my personal experience validated was liberating. It allowed me to start exploring what had happened objectively, to attack my fears of the unknown, and to find hope in moving toward creating a better life. I suddenly realized that I had choices.

The PDRs of Grieving

P—Protest. "Oh, my God, I can't believe this is happening." You're going through a phase in which your mind cannot accept something that you're going to have to accept.

D—Depression. "Oh, crap. This is really happening. It's not a bad dream. I've got to deal with this. I've got kids. I don't have the luxury of falling apart. I'm going to make it through each day. I don't know how I'm going to do it, but I don't have a choice."

R—Resolution. "Oh, well." When you've gone through this grieving phase, the thought of your divorce just stings you; it no longer knocks you off your feet.

Psychiatrist Dr. Mark Goulston, Los Angeles, California

That leads to another valuable piece of advice. If you can, see a therapist. What a therapist can do is help you navigate through this difficult time, help you get in touch with your strengths and with things that are positive in your life, and help you make decisions that are in your best interests. Grief can be a powerful, overwhelming force, but, believe it or not, divorce is actually rich in opportunity. A good therapist can help you uncover these opportunities, even in the throes of your sadness. (More on finding the right therapist, and alternatives to therapy, later in this chapter.)

Time truly does heal grief and uncover opportunity. I found the first year of separation to be the hardest. It was full of firsts. The traditions and life passages that we had celebrated as an intact family I now faced alone. Divvying up who would have the kids for the holidays and birthdays was painful. As time passed, I began to get used to the differences, planned for them, and made accommodations to my schedules and my own holidays.

This change in thinking didn't happen overnight; it took time. You grieve, you scream, and then you move on. As the saying goes, living well is the best revenge. Look toward the future and don't dwell on the past.

Fear

I was consumed with fear during my divorce. I worked through these fears, figuring out which were realistic and which were not, and tackled only those I could do something about. Do your own reality checking. Start by imagining the worst things that divorce could bring about. What would they be? What would they look like financially? What would they look like emotionally? What would they look like as a parent? Then analyze the probability that any of these things are actually going to happen. Check with your lawyer about the reality of certain fears; continue discussing them with your therapist. You may need to speak with a financial adviser or a parenting expert. Once you realistically discuss the worst possible scenarios and learn the facts, you can evaluate how likely they are to happen, and this can help you to control your worrying.

Another thing I did to control my fears was to actively imagine what my life would be like postdivorce. As this image took concrete shape, fear of the unknown began to subside, and I started to feel more comfortable with the way my life was unfolding.

Many therapists help clients reduce their fear by having them think about their past and how they survived other crises. When you think about similar times in your life when you felt pressured and survived, you begin to realize that it is possible to think, "I can get through anything."

What happens when you are going through a divorce is that you are kind of myopic. You're very focused on this. It's almost like you're a wounded animal, and you're just trying to survive, and so you really don't have a broader perspective.

Psychiatrist Dr. Mark Goulston, Los Angeles, California

What you may find overwhelming is the fear of making mistakes that are going to affect you forever. This is a scary thought. This is why it is important that you surround yourself with professionals whose expertise you trust and respect—and can afford.

Loss of Control

You may not have control over some of your choices or outcomes in divorce. For instance, you may not like that the law says that your spouse gets joint custody and has your kids during this time or that time. You may hate it. But how do you make this outcome work for you?

I started using my time on the weekends that the children spent with their father as an opportunity to pursue things that I'd rarely had the time for before. I started bike riding and boxing. Wednesday nights without the children became movie night and time to catch up with my brother and my friends. It wasn't easy not knowing what my children were doing, if their homework was being done, who they were playing with, and if they were eating healthy, balanced meals, but I realized that what I could not control I had to release. I made adjustments to my own routine to compensate for what I felt was missing.

Look at things in a more positive light, and look at what you have the ability to control. You say that your children won't survive if they are with their father every other weekend. Will they not become stronger, healthier adults if they know how to handle a relationship with someone who is difficult for them? If they learn how to deal with separation, will you not be giving the children the gift of empowerment and self-esteem, rather than burdening them with fears and trauma? Try to reframe things so they understand that they can control most of their world, and that they can handle what they can't control.

Lawyer Nancy Zalusky Berg, Walling Berg & Debele,
PA, Minneapolis, Minnesota

Lack of control can make you feel edgy. Oftentimes I felt like I'd just drunk triple shots of espresso when I hadn't touched a drop of caffeine! You might feel that your ex is trying to control you or the situation. Tunnel vision develops; you become so narrowly focused that it's difficult to see any kind of positive future, and you lose perspective.

You have to figure out what you can and can't control and can and can't let go of. So what if you don't have the energy to make dinner, and you have cereal instead? If you have children, you cannot let go of them needing clean clothes, proper meals, their bedtime routines, or a well-enforced curfew, but you can let go of whether their beds are made or their rooms are clean; you can always close the door and not look at the mess.

People who can actually visualize a better life can use that to stabilize themselves, and they're not thrown back and forth.

Psychiatrist Dr. Mark Goulston, Los Angeles, California

More Ways to Feel Better

Take Charge

What I didn't realize in those early days is that if you behave passively, like a leaf that is simply tossed this way and that by the wind, you are taking away your own freedom to move forward with your life. A smart divorce requires you to do some work, not be passive. Once you truly accept this, you will have set your feet firmly on a path that can enrich you rather than diminish you.

Give yourself the opportunity to explore and consciously make choices about the life you want to lead. There are many factors to consider. Will you have to move? Will you have to go back to work? Will you have a good life? Will you have another love in your life? Will this affect the children? How will you create your support network? Envision what you would like life to look like when you are ready to start moving on, and think about what you need to do to get there.

What happens when you can't see past this crisis? When you don't see that one day you could be part of a couple again or make a fulfilling life for yourself as a single person? Your divorce ends up taking over your life. I was consumed by my divorce. I turned down some very exciting job opportunities because I thought I didn't have time for them. In reality, I was spending hours waiting for my lawyer to call, going to court, and fretting over what may or may not happen. These were certainly not career-advancing strategies.

If you focus on the hurt you lose perspective; you lose a sense of the larger picture and how this new life can take shape. You need to develop a sense of purpose for yourself. Don't make the mistake of surrendering to your divorce by thinking, "It's the end of life." It may be the end of life as you know it now, but the truth is you could actually develop a better life if you really work at it.

Take Care of Yourself

At first, dealing with divorce can leave you so emotionally raw that you feel as if your strength is sapped. You may become tired, drained, overwhelmed, and distracted. For a while, when I was internalizing all of my problems, I suffered from severe back problems. I could not walk or sit without pain. That is why doctors will tell you that it's important to exercise during this difficult time. It's a healthy way to relieve much of the stress and pressure, and it gives you time to yourself—"adult time," as I would later come to call it. It was time I could use to escape for a while, even if it was just half an hour.

Taking care of yourself both physically and emotionally is vital to managing life and regaining health. First, take care of yourself physically—exercise, go to the gym or for a walk, eat healthfully. Second, make time for yourself—read a book, have a massage, listen to music, whatever makes you happy. There's a third way to take care of yourself during this time, and it, too, is vital: develop a support network of friends, family, clergy, parenting groups, divorce groups, and perhaps a therapist.

Finding the Right Therapist for You

My therapist helped me work through the emotional issues of divorce in much healthier ways. I had so many questions that required introspection, answers, and resolution. Picking the right therapist at this critical stage is difficult, but it's important. You will share your innermost thoughts, fantasies, fears, desires, life dreams, and so on with him or her, so choose a therapist you feel comfortable with.

There are different types of therapists and styles of therapy. For your sessions to be effective, you should have a therapist with whom you have chemistry and a comfortable relationship. If being in that person's presence feels calming, that's a feeling well worth paying attention to. If you're with a therapist and it doesn't feel right, don't stay. You can usually tell if it is a good fit after just a few sessions. Select someone who will tell you what you need to hear, not what you want to hear. Someone who will be honest with you; someone you trust and respect. You want someone who offers a balanced perspective. It needs to be someone who's not just supportive, but who takes that challenging, broader view.

You also want someone who has the professional training, is reputable, and has lots of experience with the dynamics of divorce conflict. He or she should thoroughly understand the emotions and fears that run rampant during divorce.

The easiest way to find a therapist is to check with your family doctor or lawyer for a reference. Local universities and medical schools can also provide referrals, preferably to someone who is a psychologist, psychiatrist, or social worker. If that doesn't work for you, you might want to talk to people who you know have gone through therapy themselves and ask for a reference from them.

If you feel like you can't afford therapy, look for a therapist with a sliding fee scale, or one who is covered by social services or private insurance.

Alternatives to Therapy

People deal with crises in their lives in different ways. Some people need to talk it out with a professional. Others do not have the time, resources, or inclination to do so. Still others are just very private and want to work it out on their own. The important thing is that you have to acknowledge your feelings. If you sidestep what you are going through, at some point the emotions of the experience you are facing now will surface, and they could cause problems and prevent you from moving forward.

If you're working through your emotions on your own, how you choose to do so can be a very personal decision. You have to find a coping mechanism you are comfortable with. Just make some time for yourself—time to contemplate life and just hear your feelings. Try talking it through with trusted friends or family members, writing in a journal, or reading self-help books or whatever type of book makes you feel better. Be careful who you confide in; family and friends sometimes have their own agendas. Although they are trying to be helpful, they sometimes can be really tough on you, and their advice can be unintentionally destructive. The goal is to feel better and move ahead.

Don't feel rushed into working your emotions out right away. It is going to be a confusing muddle for some time. This doesn't all resolve itself in days or weeks or even months.

Seeking Help in a Physically Abusive Situation

The issue of domestic violence is extremely serious and far too complex to be covered in a few short paragraphs or even one chapter. I do not want to treat it lightly, and I am not an expert on the topic. If you are living in this terrible circumstance, then the stakes of your divorce are that much higher, the physical and emotional pain that you face is far greater, and the need for a support system to help you through this time and maintain your sanity is that much more urgent. You can reach out to mental health professionals, support organizations, and the courts for assistance in helping you seek safety.

- **Mental health professionals.** Look for someone who has training and competency in working with the dynamics of domestic violence and abuse. You may find someone with the appropriate training and understanding through your lawyer or family doctor.

- **Women's shelters.** If you are in an abusive, violent relationship, you may seek refuge in a shelter for a period of time (see "Resources," page 190).
- **The court system.** You can use the courts to obtain a restraining order or a no contact order.

Domestic violence and high conflict are two different categories. *Domestic violence* involves a relationship in which there is criminal behavior. It's usually the man assaulting the woman. That is a very particular dynamic that affects everything in the family. It affects the parents, it affects the children, and it affects how the case works. *High conflict* pertains to a family who is still really fighting and really engaged with each other. It's also their way of having contact with each other and control over each other and influence over each other's lives; they are not at all disengaged from each other. High-conflict families result in a disproportionate expenditure of time in our justice system, in our law offices, in mediator offices. They take up resources. Lots of these families are just ordinary, middle-class people who are just so damn angry they are just not able to move on.

Lawyer Carole Curtis, Carole Curtis Law Offices, Toronto, Ontario

---

Now that you understand that you are not alone in your feelings and grief and know how to take care of yourself, it is important for those of you with children to look at what your kids are experiencing and how you can help them.

3

Parenting Throughout Divorce

Temper tantrums, withdrawal, regression, anger, sadness . . . just as you, the parent, experience so many mixed emotions, so do your children.

There has been a lot of research that's looked at the adjustment of children to divorce. The data suggest that probably 70–75 percent of kids going through the divorce process end up making a reasonable adaptation to the dissolution of the family and a year and a half later are indistinguishable from kids whose families are not divorced. But 20–30 percent of the kids get significantly symptomatic and seem to have difficulty coping with the divorce, the parents, or the dissolution of the family. A number of factors have been identified to help predict whether kids will adjust well. Conflict exposure is by far the most powerful predictor of difficulty.

Psychologist Dr. Bruce Copeland, Bethesda, Maryland

Telling Your Children About Your Divorce

Telling my seven-year-old son that his parents were separating was gut wrenching. This was one of the first times in my life when I was really at a loss for words. As impulsive as I tend to be, I knew that this was one occasion that really required thought in advance. I knew that whatever I said, it was important to say it right, and at my son's level. It was incredibly difficult to tell him that his life was about to change.

I sought help by speaking with a parenting expert, who advised me to say something along the lines of "Mommy and Daddy have adult problems. You will be fine, your brother and sister (one and three years old at the time) will be fine, and we love you. We are still a family; you just won't have your parents living in the same home." My son became very quiet and wanted to be alone. I hugged him for a very long time and we sat together, a memory I will never forget.

Here are some tips from the experts on telling your kids about your divorce:

- Talk to the children together.
- Give children time to react and time to be mad and sad, and to ask questions. If you have more than one child, each may want to speak with you separately.
- Try to anticipate the children's questions and reactions, and be prepared to respond.
- Encourage your children to talk about their feelings.

What children need is:

- to feel loved
- to realize that it's not their fault

- a sense of security
- for parents to make decisions
- routine and structure
- not to be put in the middle

Children do live out the divorce. It does become their life. Some parents feel guilty that they didn't give their kids the same life that they had themselves. The life of a child of a divorced family can be a good life, a happy life, and one full of happy memories. The parents' job is to give the child a childhood, but some kids from divorced families lose their childhood, not just because of the divorce but because the parents don't manage their parenting and the relationship with their ex well. That's why I don't like the label "child of divorce." It makes it seem like that is who the child is, and it is not. Kids are kids, and we need to work on making divorce less hard for them as they grow. I don't want them to see themselves as having lived their lives under the shadow. I want them to see themselves as kids first.

Professor of Psychology Dr. Robert E. Emery, Director, Center for Children, Families, and the Law, University of Virginia, Charlottesville, Virginia

---

The reasons behind your divorce are likely not relevant to your children and should not be shared. Very often one of the parents feels wounded and thinks, "I'm not going to lie to the children about this divorce. I'm not going to tell them that I want this to happen when I don't. They need to know the truth." But who is this information really helping? It will only confuse the children, may destroy their relationship with their other parent, and could have a monumental impact emotionally. You have to be aware of your own feelings so that you don't say too much; you need to be careful. If you feel the urge to say something you shouldn't, leave the room. Write out what you wish you could say (which can also be cathartic), try deep breathing, or vent to a trusted friend.

To relieve some of your children's anxiety, be prepared to answer questions such as the following:

- Where are we going to be living?
- How much time am I going to be spending with each of you?
- Am I going to keep my friends?
- Will I be going to the same school?

Having these answers ready will give your children a sense of security. It will give them the message that their parents have worked things out, that lots of things are going to remain constant, and that it's going to be OK.

Families need good family health. This means that:
- parents are present, and are not distracted from attending to their children
- children are able to express appropriate egocentrism—they are not "taking care" of their parents
- individual family members have energy and attention for daily and long-term developmental tasks and goals, and children move unimpeded through their development

Psychologist Dr. Wendy Hutchins-Cook, Seattle, Washington

What Your Children Are Going Through

Quite honestly, I never really thought of my children grieving my divorce. I knew they were going to experience the loss of our family as they knew it. I knew that divorce would have a profound impact on their lives. But, until I started my research for this book,

I didn't fully comprehend the extent of what my children were experiencing. My oldest son often tells me, "Mom, you don't know how I am feeling because you grew up with two parents at home." He is right; it is difficult for me to understand at times. What I have learned is to try to visualize myself in my child's situation to see what he or she may be experiencing, especially when the conflict is high.

What can you do to help your child during this time when they are experiencing their own Rocky Mountain blues?

- Try to step inside your child's world and really imagine what life looks like from his or her perspective, not from yours.
- If you're not sure how your children are feeling, openly discuss it with them. Brainstorm with friends or your therapist the kinds of questions to ask in order to find out how your child sees his or her own world.
- Make sure that your child has somebody neutral to speak to, someone who thinks well of both parents—perhaps a trusted friend or your child's own therapist.

Child therapist Diane Moody, McWhinney Metcalfe
and Associates, Toronto, Ontario

Just as you may feel alone during this time, children also feel very alone in their experiences. While many parents confide in friends, most children do not. Many children do not have the intellectual or emotional maturity, the verbal skills, or the life experience to cope with this change in family status. They take their signals from their parents. If one parent is stressed, disorganized, and depressed, that often becomes alarming to their children. Alternatively, if a parent is unruffled and composed, this has a calming and reassuring effect. We often don't give our children enough credit for reading our moods.

Smart Tips on Parenting Throughout Divorce

- Parents need to parent so that kids can be kids, not children of divorce.
- Parents need to recognize their own emotions.
- Parents need to recognize that divorce is a hard and emotional time for the children.
- Children bounce back, but that doesn't mean that the bounce doesn't hurt.
- How parents parent and what parents do—that determines how resilient children are and how they bounce back from the effects of divorce.

Professor of Psychology Dr. Robert E. Emery, Director, Center for Children, Families, and the Law, University of Virginia, Charlottesville, Virginia

Their reaction to divorce also depends on what the history has been. If there has been a fair amount of family conflict, it may actually be a relief when separation occurs. Even though they may be in shock at the beginning, if the conflict levels are lowered, children end up doing better in the long run.

Parental conflict is one of the hardest things for children, perhaps even harder than divorce itself.

Psychologist Dr. Souhir Benhamida, Seattle, Washington

Another factor that affects how children cope with divorce is their age at the time of separation. A toddler is only going to be aware of the presence or absence of a parent, stress or tension, or the parent's crying or being angry, whereas a teenager is going to understand the situation more fully. Keep in mind, however, that the way your children behave is not always a reaction to the divorce; it may instead be a function of the stage of life they are at. For example, teenagers are difficult at the best of times; they are constantly trying to assert their independence. Their attitude may have nothing at all to do with your separation.

Children need to learn to grieve in their own way and in their own rhythm. So you have to create an environment where the children are comfortable looking at how they feel, but also not feeling that they are required to look at how they feel.

Psychologist Dr. Jonathan W. Gould, Charlotte, North Carolina

---

Putting Your Children's Best Interests First

Most people love their children more than they despise the other parent, and they understand that parental conflict hurts children. The problem is puncturing through the hurt, fear, and anger that you are feeling to keep focused on the need to put your children first.

Your mission as a parent is to focus on your goals for your children and how best to attain these goals—for example, educational goals or your relationship together. Your duty as a parent is to raise your children in the best way possible, supporting them both financially and emotionally.

Psychologist Dr. Peggy Thompson, Family Psychological Services,
Orinda, California

Parents often become self-centered during divorce, particularly during the first year, because they are dealing with so much.

Some parents are so caught up in their own grief that they end up projecting much greater distress onto their children. Others are so anxious to make everything better for their children that they don't give them the space they need to grieve. But to be an effective parent during this time, you have to put your own emotions on the shelf, at least temporarily, and help your children with theirs.

If the parent cannot shift from focusing on his own needs or desire to "get back at" the other parent, the child suffers. On the other hand, when the parent is able to look at the situation from the child's point of view, he is in a much better position to meet the child's needs.

A woman is devastated to learn that her husband is leaving her for another woman. If she were to act out her feelings, she might berate her husband to her daughter, perhaps hoping that the child will side with her and not her husband. If instead she is able to put herself in her daughter's shoes, then she might hold back expressing her anger in front of her daughter, realizing that were she to do so, her child would feel pulled between the parents. On the one hand, she would feel the need to side with her betrayed mother; on the other hand, she would want to protect and defend her father, whom she also loves.

Social worker Elinor Gertner, Jewish Family and Child Service,
Toronto, Ontario

Putting my children's best interests first was sometimes difficult, especially when I was dealing with my own issues with my ex. Being the bigger person and looking the other way wasn't always easy. As time went on, I began to take my lawyer's advice: "Don't engage." I didn't get sucked into battle, as this was not a war to be won. Holding my head up high, taking the high road, and doing what I knew was in my children's best interests contributed to their positive emotional health. The goal is not to punish the other parent; the goal is to let your children have the best life possible.

Divorce represents a loss for almost everyone it touches. As difficult as it is for parents, at least they have perspective. This is not true for children. In fact, for most children, divorce will be the first major crisis of their lives. Still, most children have to adapt to life in two households. However, every child needs to have the sense that even though many things have changed, one thing remains constant: Mom and Dad can still be counted on to be there, whenever that might be. When children feel secure in that, they can shift the focus of their daily lives back to where it belongs: on being a kid, on their activities, friends, and routines.

Professor of Psychology Dr. Robert E. Emery, Director, Center for Children, Families, and the Law, University of Virginia, Charlottesville, Virginia; from his book The Truth About Children and Divorce *(New York: Viking Adult, 2004)*

There are many ways to learn about parenting skills and putting your children's best interests first: reading books on parenting or on the effects of divorce on children; taking courses at your local community center; or getting help from social services organizations (see "Resources," page 187). There are parenting specialists, organizations that focus on divorced families, and, of course, therapists with the same focus.

If there are any signs of unexpected or unexplained changes in your children's behavior, you may want to consider having them speak with a therapist or other neutral third party (someone who won't side with one parent or the other). Some examples of the behavioral changes to watch out for are a sudden drop in school performance, altered sleep patterns, not spending time with friends, and becoming withdrawn.

Now that you know that neither you nor your children are alone in your feelings throughout divorce, that there are steps you can take to help yourself and people you can rely on to help you as well, it is time to take control of your divorce! Understanding exactly what your divorce options are is the first step.

4

Considering All
the Divorce Options

G oing into my divorce, I didn't realize there were any options. Maybe I watched too much TV, but my perception was that everyone went to court and litigated—went to trial before a judge. I was completely wrong. I didn't understand that litigation is not the preferred method of resolution. All lawyers would agree that in most situations, it is the method of last resort; it usually signals a breakdown in negotiations outside the courtroom. The other options besides litigation are called alternative dispute resolutions, or ADRs.

The newest thinking is not that litigation is the standard and everything else is "alternative dispute resolution," or ADR. The best-practices thinking is that ADR ought to mean "appropriate dispute resolution," of which litigation is one choice.

Lawyer Carren S. Oler, Law Office of
Carren S. Oler, Rockville, Maryland

Understanding each ADR process is vitally important. Although no one should walk into a lawyer's office and immediately say, "I

want dispute resolution X"—lawyers evaluate which dispute resolution process to pursue based on the nature of the problems and
issues—being aware of your choices can help you maintain control
and contribute to making decisions with confidence.

Which option provides the best outcome? All of these modalities can produce either a good outcome or a bad one. Mediation, arbitration, trial—
nothing about them, alone, predicts either a good or bad outcome. All
carry variables such as a good judge or a bad judge, a good mediator or
a bad mediator, a good lawyer or a bad lawyer. When you, the lawyer,
spend hours with your client, you can then effectively recommend the
best process for your client. There needs to be an understanding of process
because, as always, information is power.

Lawyer Glenn C. Lewis, Lewis Law Firm, Washington, D.C.

Here then, are the six divorce processes—what they are, how
they work, and their advantages and disadvantages.

The Do-It-Yourself Divorce

Divorce pro se is also known as a "kitchen table agreement" or a
"do-it-yourself" divorce. This system—in which divorcing couples
draw up their own agreement, without the help of a lawyer, and
present it to a judge to sign—is becoming popular. Many couples
choose to handle their own divorce because they feel that the lawyer's fees are just too expensive. This route requires a tremendous
ability to communicate, a low level of conflict, a high level of trust
(both parties must ensure that they receive complete financial disclosure from the other side), and virtually no assets to divide.

Some people do an excellent job of drawing up their own agreement. However, others fail to represent themselves wisely. Even
for those who research and become familiar with their rights and

responsibilities, emotions can get in the way and cause significant problems.

Divorce pro se is fine if you have a relatively younger, shorter marriage. If you're talking about a couple of graduate students, and the estate is relatively small, and there are no children. But family law can get complicated, and it is easy to make a mistake. It is easy in a *pro se* situation for one party to say, "I am not giving you my retirement plan," and the retirement plan might be the biggest asset that person has. Discuss what your rights are and what the probable outcome is with a lawyer. Then you can go and negotiate, but at least you know what you have, what you can give up, and what you shouldn't give up.

Lawyer Geoff Hamilton, Char Hamilton
Campbell & Yoshida, Honolulu, Hawaii

Family law is fact specific. Everybody has their story to tell, and the stories are all variations of the same ten things. But the variations make a difference in what you're going to do, and that's why I don't recommend trying to negotiate your own divorce.

Lawyer Judith E. Siegel-Baum, Wolf, Block, Schorr
and Solis-Cohen, LLP, New York, New York

If this route is pursued, you may first want to talk to a lawyer. You should also consider taking the final document to a lawyer for an opinion prior to signing. You and your spouse need to use separate and independent lawyers who can advise each of you of your respective rights and obligations without fear of a conflict of interest. For instance, a lawyer who represented your spouse in the past should not be advising you in the current situation.

Negotiation

In the negotiation approach to divorce, each spouse draws up a resolution that he or she thinks is fair, including a wish list regarding the division of assets, parenting responsibilities, and visitation rights, and shares the proposal with the other party. The two proposals are considered the starting point, and the couple go back and forth adjusting them, in the hopes of reaching an acceptable middle ground. Negotiation requires that both parties discuss the situation in a reasonable manner. If one person says, "Here's my bottom line. Take it or leave it, and if you don't take it, I'll see you in court," that doesn't allow the other person to stay in the process.

If both parties retain lawyers, the agreement is negotiated through lawyers' letters or four-way meetings. If you are lucky, you can negotiate the terms on your own, without lawyers, and then finalize the agreement through the lawyers.

The negotiation process is also used in mediation and collaborative law, and in most instances within the litigation process, in order to preclude the need for an actual trial.

In my world, everything starts with the negotiation process. The moment you bring third parties in, whether it's courts, mediators, or arbitrators, you're adding cost, you're adding delay, you're adding another layer. So my first letter to the other side is always, "Come negotiate with me." Sometimes people say "Drop dead." But more often than not, the lawyer will say, "Let's see what we can do."

Lawyer Lorne Wolfson, Torkin Manes, Toronto, Ontario

There are different negotiation styles, and the style used by your legal counsel will depend in part on his or her legal philosophy and on the form of dispute resolution you're pursuing. In *rights-based* or *distributed-based negotiation,* a fixed pool of funds is divided between the parties, each of whom is trying to negotiate as big a share as he or she is entitled to. In *interest-based negotiation,* the strategy used by collaborative lawyers (see "Collaborative Law," below), the separating couple divides the pool of funds based not on what each person is entitled to but on what each one needs.

A classic example of interest-based negotiation would be a father who wants more time with his children, and a mother who is terrified that if he has the kids more than 40 percent of the time, she may lose financially through reduced child support. A resolution may be achieved by the father saying, "I'll pay the full amount of guideline support; I just want more time." Everyone goes away with their goals having been met.

Collaborative Family Lawyer Sharon Cohen, Dickson MacGregor Appell, LLP, Toronto, Ontario

---

Hard bargaining is a very adversarial way of negotiating that combines a take-it-or-leave-it attitude with bluffs, threats, and the withholding of information. The goal is to win at all costs. *Soft bargaining* is the opposite technique, in which the negotiator tries to avoid confrontation and to preserve some civil relationship between the former spouses. Individuals engaged in soft bargaining are more likely to compromise and share information.

Every person is different, each person is different from moment to moment, and every breakup is different. Often, people engage in power bargaining because they are afraid, or are feeling "powered-down," or think that if they don't, they will become soft and not get what they need, or because that was how they negotiated during their marriage, and their whole relationship was based on power contests. But power contests generate a great deal of "collateral damage," create winners and losers, and draw future disputes in their wake. Instead, divorcing spouses may use rights-based methods such as litigation, or adversarial negotiations, which create limitations on the exercise of power but still result in winners and losers and lesser versions of all the problems created by power contests. But interest-based processes such as mediation and collaborative negotiation focus on identifying the reasons people seek power or rights, and they try to reveal and resolve the underlying reasons that generated the conflict. Interest-based processes require couples to say not only what they want but also why they want it, and encourage them to communicate at a deeper level, learn from each other, and work collaboratively to resolve their disputes.

Mediator and lawyer Kenneth Cloke, Center for Dispute
Resolution, Santa Monica, California

Mediation

Mediation involves using third-party intervention as a way for the parties to negotiate the divorce agreement outside the courtroom. The role of the mediator is to help the couple identify issues and explore available choices. A mediator must be neutral, fair, just, and impartial. The purpose of mediation is to help the separating couple arrive at an agreement they can both live with, rather than having a decision imposed upon them by a third party (such as a judge or arbitrator). This gives both sides more control over the resolution, but it requires that they be willing to compromise.

Mediators do not offer legal advice or advocate for either party. Therefore, each party should seek the opinion of independent legal counsel as well, either before mediation begins or once an agreement has been reached but before it's signed. Sometimes lawyers prefer being involved in the actual mediation process, and other times it is not required. Only you can really determine what is important to you and what that is worth. Is it really necessary and cost-effective to have your lawyer help you figure out every third sleepover? On the other hand, does your parenting plan have financial implications that you're not qualified to figure out by yourself?

In mediation, you are trying to reduce emotion with clients because it's emotion that is actually getting in the way of them making good judgment. Would you trust any of the people you know going through divorce with any decisions that they are going to make if they were highly emotional?

Mediator Dr. Larry Fong, Fong Mediate, Calgary, Alberta

How to Choose a Mediator

What makes a good mediator? When choosing your mediator, make sure he or she:

- asks questions to encourage the separating couple to come to decisions on their own in a way that they did not think about before
- is a good listener; hears what the couple say and what they don't say
- understands the emotional issues involved
- understands the legal obligations of the jurisdiction in which the separating couple are mediating
- helps the couple to trust the process
- helps them to focus on what is in the best interests of the children

We say that a good administrator is one that you don't even know is there. It's also true with a mediator. It's not that I'm the expert on your relationship, but that I'm here to help the two of you talk to each other. Normally, you could talk and solve your problems, but because of the pain of the divorce you need some help to restore some open lines of communication and some constructive conversations between you. And that's where the real skill in mediation is—in helping people make the emotional shift from blame and arguing about whose fault this is to recognizing that each party has contributed to what happened.

Mediator Dr. Carl D. Schneider, PhD, Mediation
Matters, Bethesda, Maryland

There are different mediation models; the one that's used depends upon the philosophy and training of the mediator. A mediator may be a lawyer, or a mental health professional such as a psychologist or social worker. Some mediators have a more therapeutic style and work toward both of the individuals being emotionally ready to separate. Some mediate just financial issues or strictly parenting issues, while others will handle both. Do your own research to find the right mediator for you. After all, you want a sense of comfort, and you want to be able to live with the outcome without feeling pushed into the results.

Should your mediator be a lawyer or a mental health professional? The answer to this depends on what the issues are. If you're negotiating financial issues, lawyers prefer that the mediator also be a lawyer, because that is their training; they understand the financial intricacies of things and can perform the analyses that are sometimes necessary. In addition, they understand what is likely to happen if the case goes to court.

If you're negotiating custody issues or preparing a detailed parenting plan, most lawyers would advise you to choose a mental health professional as a mediator. You'll be relying on the mediator for information about what is in the best interests of the children, and in most cases that is not a lawyer-mediator's area of expertise. However, if you and your spouse are not engaged in high conflict and your negotiating positions are not too far apart, lawyers would agree that it is not inappropriate for a lawyer to mediate parenting issues as well.

You really need to evaluate these options carefully, in consultation with your legal counsel. Do your own due diligence.

When Does Mediation Not Work?

In order for mediation to be successful, it requires the will of the persons involved to come to an agreement. Both parties must agree to participate in mediation and sign the mediation agreement. They must commit to the disclosure of all pertinent information and focus on the best interests of the children. In cases in which that will is not there, lawyers do not usually recommend mediation. For instance, if someone is refusing to pay spousal or child support or is withholding financial information, then you need to consider another form of dispute resolution.

You should consult your lawyer if you're concerned about a power imbalance in mediation. Some people feel that they cannot articulate their issues as well as their spouse, or that they're not as financially savvy. Others worry because their spouse has all of the financial resources and they have next to nothing. Many mediators feel that they can help individuals work through these imbalances, but not every mediator is skilled in handling them. Consider your options carefully.

Most mediators will not take on cases in which domestic violence has been involved. Lastly, some lawyers would argue that you cannot mediate when one party wants to move away with the children and it is permissible by the court.

What about when a couple can't sit in the same room together? A skilled mediator can still assist a couple in coming to an agreement when they are sitting in separate rooms. This is when the mediator gets a physical workout, going back and forth between the rooms; this is called *caucusing*. When you don't trust your spouse, a skilled mediator makes it his or her job to help clients trust in the process. Bring a good magazine or book for the downtime when the mediator is with your spouse.

Closed Versus Open Mediation

In a *closed mediation*, whatever is discussed or whatever offers are made in the mediation process, the outcomes and conversations remain private. There is no written report. In an *open mediation*, there is a written report that could be admissible in court.

If there's a really unusual problem, or sexual matters that have to be discussed, and these issues shouldn't be openly disclosed to the public, the preference might be for closed mediation. But in the ordinary family law case, lawyers generally prefer open mediation. If an open mediation breaks down (which certainly does happen), the mediator can write a report as to what was agreed to, what wasn't, and each party's position, and this report can facilitate further discussion and protect the parties from being quoted out of context or incorrectly. The problem with closed mediation is that if it's unsuccessful, you have to start all over again.

If mediation breaks down and there is no resolution, in most instances the next step would be arbitration or litigation. Both are discussed later in this chapter.

Collaborative Law

Collaborative law was created in 1991 by Stuart Webb, a lawyer in Minneapolis, Minnesota. The concept is that the lawyers work strictly toward settlement. Clients and their lawyers sign a contract in which they agree not to go to court, and to provide full and complete financial disclosure. The purpose of collaborative law is to create an environment in which the separating couple feels safe, in which both parties feel that they are able to make informed decisions about their own destinies, and in which they can work constructively despite their fears, anger, and feelings of revenge.

The lawyers fulfill their traditional role of advising their own clients on how the law applies to their individual situations. But they also help their clients to reframe their thinking—to develop goals as opposed to taking positions, and to make good and ethical choices. When the divorcing spouses meet, their lawyers are at their sides to help them conduct interest-based negotiations based on needs, not rights, and to work toward a parenting and financial plan that is acceptable to both clients. If either client wishes to end the collaborative process and go to court, both lawyers and other members of their firms must remove themselves from the case.

If settlement is difficult to achieve, a team of specialists is formed to help the separating couple through the process. Specialists can include the following:

- **Divorce coach.** A divorce coach may be retained by each of the separating spouses to ease communication, diffuse any conflict, and help them individually deal with the impact of the divorce. The coaches are mental health professionals who are specialized in helping the family, but whereas therapists try to help people change or look at their past, divorce coaches are focused on the goals of their clients and their families, and on how to attain those goals.
- **Child specialist.** This is a neutral third party who will work with the parents to help them understand their children's needs and wishes. This person is the voice of the children, and may meet with them. He or she may develop a comprehensive parenting plan to attach to the separation agreement.
- **Financial professional.** Also a neutral third party, this professional provides advice and assistance regarding the financial settlement.

The Benefits and Limitations of Collaborative Law

Collaborative law helps clients work through their issues at a pace they both find comfortable. The team approach helps to defuse differences and to keep the focus on the children's best interests. And the fact that there's no option to litigate frequently produces constructive settlements.

In order for it to work, however, both parties must agree to participate, and both must sign the contract that removes the possibility of litigation from the process. They must commit to full financial disclosure and exhibit mutual respect and honesty. Each must retain a collaborative lawyer.

If you are trying to keep legal fees to a minimum, the expense of the specialists involved can be prohibitive. Not all lawyers are supportive of the process, and the no-litigation agreement means that if a settlement is not reached, your lawyers must withdraw and you must retain new representation. (Collaborative lawyers may assist in the transfer of files.)

Collaborative law is not practiced in all states. To find a complete list of collaborative professionals by state, county, or province, visit the International Academy of Collaborative Professionals Web site: www.collaborativepractice.com (also listed in "Resources," page 187.

Arbitration

Arbitration is much like litigation in that you go to "court," in a sense, but it is outside the court system. Arbitration is a private process in which the divorcing spouses, together with their lawyers, pick a decision maker, who is usually a retired judge or senior lawyer and who will likely have family law expertise, to decide the issues in question (financial, child-related, and so forth). Many lawyers like this option because it gives them some control over the selection of the "judge"; with litigation, the court assigns the judge, who might not necessarily be a family law specialist.

The typical arbitration is less formal than a court proceeding, but you can have whatever degree of formality you want. You can have a court reporter there. You can call witnesses, request evidence from your spouse, and submit your own evidence. The bottom line, though, is that once both sides of the case are presented to the arbitrator, it is his or her job to come to a decision on what the divorce agreement should look like. In most instances the arbitrator's decision is binding (legally enforceable) and cannot be appealed, though this depends on the arbitration rules of the state or jurisdiction in which the separating couple resides. In most cases the cost of arbitration is shared by the separating couple, who must also sign an arbitration agreement.

Arbitration for divorce settlements or for divorces that involve children may be unavailable in some states or jurisdictions. Ask your lawyer if it is an option in your area.

The Benefits and Limitations of Arbitration

Arbitration is usually faster and less expensive than litigation, because there is no waiting around for the court schedule to open up, and no going through court proceedings such as settlement conferences. Arbitration is private, meaning there is no public record of the dispute. It's usually less adversarial than litigation, and your case is the focus of the arbitrator, whereas in court yours might be one of many cases handled during that day by the presiding judge.

Lawyers don't typically recommend arbitration when one member of the couple involved has absolutely no regard for the rule of law—for instance, when one party is reluctant to make full disclosure and requires the other person's lawyer to make a lot of extra motions to get that information through the system. It is believed that these individuals need the authority of the judge to control the process, which is different than the authority of the arbitrator. An experienced arbitrator might run a better trial, but he or she does not have the same power as the court. In addition, some people will pay more attention to a judge than they will to an arbitrator. If you know in advance that your former partner is dishonest or deceptive, then there probably should not be any arbitration.

Arbitration is also not usually recommended when there are very complex financial details, many witnesses to be called, or two very different legal issues to be resolved (for example, a child-related disagreement and a financial dispute).

Some lawyers are not supportive of this method of dispute resolution in general. Since it usually requires you to give up your right to appeal a decision you disagree with, it can be argued that there are no checks and balances on the arbitrator's power, and that this puts less pressure on the arbitrator to be fair and to be governed by the law. These concerns must be carefully discussed with your lawyer.

Mediation/Arbitration

There are some mediators that act as arbitrators as well. If a mediation/arbitration agreement is signed at the beginning of the mediation process and the mediation breaks down, the mediator then assumes the role of an arbitrator. Some would say that if there is an impasse and one side is being unreasonable, then you need a third party to break the deadlock. But you need someone who is highly skilled to be able to serve both functions. And while this switch in roles is sometimes necessary, it is only appropriate if the parties were fully informed at the beginning of the process and understand the implications of the potential switch, because information disclosed to the mediator will be used in a different manner once the mediator changes roles and becomes the arbitrator.

This option is not offered in all states or jurisdictions for divorce settlements or those involving children. Ask your lawyer if it's a possibility in your area.

Nine times out of ten, when you're in what I call mediation/arbitration with a good mediator/arbitrator, you never get into the arbitration. But you need that club over people's heads to get them to go that last little mile to make the deal. A good mediator/arbitrator is very effective in doing that.

Lawyer Lorne Wolfson, Torkin Manes, Toronto, Ontario

Many more people are going to mediation accompanied by their lawyers, who try to work through their difficulties and assist them in achieving a reasonable result, which is quite civilized. You can always have arbitration or hire a private judge. You can also negotiate between opposing counsel and end up with an agreement. On the other hand, there are just some people who are going to fight no matter what, and they do that in a courtroom.

Lawyer Nicholas A. Leto Jr., Veltmann & Leto, LLP, San Diego, California

Litigation

A divorce may be litigated for a number of reasons. Perhaps resolving matters by one of the means described above has not worked, and now there is only one alternative: to reach a resolution by going to court. Perhaps one party has no money for legal fees, has had to deal with abuse, or is just plain angry, and wants to start the litigation process right away, without attempting another method first.

The litigation process begins when your or your ex's lawyer issues a claim—a formal *application for divorce* (known as a *petition for divorce* in some jurisdictions) and/or a demand for money, property, or the enforcement of legal rights. The official request for divorce and the various legal demands may exist as separate legal proceedings—for instance, a spouse may sue for custody of the children without first filing for divorce.

Once the claim is issued, it becomes part of a newly created trial record, which will also include the other party's response to the claim, as well as any relevant financial documents and court orders. If nothing else happens, then maybe a year later the judge will read the documents in the trial record and the trial will commence—the lawyers will present your case, and so on.

Most people can't just sit around and wait a year or more for the trial to begin; usually, there are issues that require immediate attention. If, for example, you separated and your financially aware spouse walked out the front door without leaving you any money to pay the mortgage, you couldn't wait until your day in court to arrange for support payments. In most jurisdictions, your first opportunity to arrange these payments would be at a *case conference*, an initial intervention through which the court attempts to isolate and resolve especially pressing issues. If you couldn't resolve the issue at the case conference, then you would be permitted to bring an *interim motion* for support payment. The purpose of the interim order is to get you through until trial.

Once the case conference and the interim motions are out of the way, the lawyers can begin taking the sworn statements of witnesses; these statements are called *depositions* or *discoveries*. (The terms vary by jurisdiction, but in principle the processes are very similar.) Depositions and discoveries provide an understanding of the case that you have to make at trial and ensure that both sides have all the information they are entitled to.

Then there are settlement conferences, adjournments, and so on. If you do end up going through with the trial itself, it can last for as little as a day or run on for weeks. The whole process feels like an eternity when you're in it.

When you do litigate, do it swiftly and win so that it doesn't prolong the agony. *Quickly* is a relative term in litigation, but winning quickly brings closure. You want to prepare the client for that, you want to plan through to closure. Litigation, done appropriately, can actually bring closure to people's problems when other things fail.

Lawyer Mike McCurley, McCurley Orsinger McCurley
Nelson & Downing, LLP, Dallas, Texas

But of all the cases that end up in court, only 5 percent of these go all the way to a full-blown trial. The lawyers' typical strategy is to use the threat of trial to get people to bargain and settle. Have you heard the expression "in the shadow of the courthouse"? These few words capture the essence of the threat. There is an expectation that there will be some maneuvering and bargaining and, eventually, a settlement. Settlements may be reached in various ways; the way the courts handle such situations differs by state, jurisdiction, and judge.

The trial, for most people, is like a supercharged cattle prod. They don't want to go there. So it is always advisable to keep negotiating and negotiating. There have been many cases where we have settled on the footstep of the door to the court house. There have been cases where we have settled after one or two witnesses have presented their evidence. We've settled cases while a judge has reserved his or her decision. You settle cases sometimes in a week or two and sometimes many months or years later. One thing you never do is give up hope, because you are always looking for that time that's right for both sides.

Lawyer Jim Stoffman, Taylor McCaffrey, Winnipeg, Manitoba

The thing that produces the settlement is to always keep moving toward the finish line. I move toward settlement passionately, and I move toward trial passionately. I don't stop on either track. I'm always moving toward trial while watching for opportunities to settle. You usually utilize both the carrot and the stick, offering the opponent an incentive, a good reason to settle. In most instances, you thread the needle by establishing his or her risk if going to trial without ever giving away your winning hand if they do so. If you fail to prepare a winning case, you will need to try the case. This may sound counterintuitive, but it never fails to prove true. This is nothing less than the logical extension of the Cold War doctrine of "peace through strength." To maintain peace with the Soviets, we needed to prove to them that we could win and were willing to do so. In the context of divorce practice, this means you often must be aggressive to have peace.

Lawyer Glenn C. Lewis, Lewis Law Firm, Washington, D.C.

Emotional Aspects of Litigation

Litigation can be a tense and emotionally charged process. It is definitely the least amicable of the options described; that's why litigation is also known as "the adversarial process." Litigation polarizes people because this is a zero-sum game; there's one winner and one loser. It's his word against hers. Your gladiators—your lawyers—go to war for you. They both try to show why their client is the better person, and why the other side is unfit or unbalanced, or has some other serious deficiency. (I am not referring to those times when the accusations are indeed factual, scary, and sad.) The impact on the family can be disastrous. If each side's tactic is to try to make the other look bad, most likely things will be said that will destroy the possibility of any kind of amicable relationship later on. Words can never be taken back.

The divorce system itself can be a crazy-making system. There's a typical phrase that people say in the court: "People in criminal court are bad people on their best behavior, and people in family court are good people on their worst behavior." Although many parents don't actually have personality disorders, they may manifest traits of such disorders in this crazy system because there's so much emotion around the courts—law, shame, fear, and anger.

Psychologist Dr. Philip M. Stahl, Gilbert, Arizona

Dr. Robert Emery, Professor of Psychology and Director of the Center for Children, Families, and the Law at the University of Virginia, conducted a study examining the effects of divorce mediation versus litigation on the relationship that nonresident parents had with their children. Divorcing couples were randomly assigned to either mediate or litigate their differences. Twelve years later, 28 percent of the nonresident parents who had mediated saw their children weekly, compared to 9 percent of those who litigated. So, although litigation is sometimes necessary, it is important to be aware of the potential results that can affect your family. Litigation is hard on everybody.

Family law litigation involves emotion. Indeed, it is a bit like the battle that it unofficially represents. The heart quickens as the court date comes. And, when you are actually litigating, you're actually battling. I'm sure every divorce lawyer will tell you how many times they get a copy of their opponent's sworn declaration, with their client's handwritten "that's a lie" in the margin. The fact is, clients are presented with things that most of us never have to face: sworn statements about you or about things you've done that are set up in the public record. That is enough to get you emotional. You need to control and try to channel that emotion, but it is difficult.

Appellate lawyer Paige Leslie Wickland,
Fancher & Wickland, San Francisco, California

It's also important to remember that what you will get with litigation is the decision of a judge and the brand of justice that the courts like to give out. It may or may not be your brand of justice. You may be very unhappy with the end result, which may not be in your favor, and then you may feel that there has been no justice at all. As much as you are hoping for vindication, there never really is any, which could leave you frustrated, disappointed, and disillusioned.

Contrary to popular belief and the Hollywood view, court is not about finding the truth. It is about perception. The perception of one man or woman—the judge. As a human being with limited knowledge, and limited time to collect facts, the judge is only able to make decisions based upon what is presented. Don't expect your lawyer to turn everything around at the last minute, Perry Mason–like, by making your soon-to-be ex-spouse break down on the stand.

Mediator and lawyer William A. Eddy, National Conflict Resolution Center, San Diego, California

---

Talk to your lawyer to get a sense of the emotional side of litigation. This is also a good time to turn to your therapist or a trusted confidant for emotional support.

Litigation Insights and Advice

- Remember that the trial lawyers are not necessarily seeking the truth. They are trying to "win" the battle (not solve the problem) by limiting any evidence that diminishes their side of the case and by expanding any that enhances it. The real goal is to push the rules of evidence as far as possible to show only their client's side. In today's litigious environment, some parties show little or no hesitation in slanting or avoiding the facts in their efforts to win.

- In serving as a judge in over fifteen hundred cases, I have never seen a "winner." The adversarial process is financially and emotionally draining and leads to permanent embitterment. Nothing about the judicial process offers emotional support. It is simply not a function of the court.

- The pace and pressure of trial runs counter to good decision making. After sitting outside a pretrial conference (between lawyers and the judge) in an emotional state, where you can't decide whether you want Diet Coke or iced tea to drink, your lawyer emerges and says, "You have five minutes to decide if you want to keep the house or sell the house." To avoid having a trial, you have to make one of your biggest choices at a time when you are least emotionally equipped to make a decision.

- If litigation appears to be your only option (it really rarely is), make sure you know about the judge assigned to your case. He or she is human, subject to bias and prejudice, and is now in control of your case. A good lawyer will know what the judge likes and what to expect. Remember, the judge is not there to protect you, only to apply the law to the facts as they are presented in court.

- The major roadblock to amicable resolution in a litigated case is that the traditional approach offers no exit route. Once you start down the path, developing and delivering the negative comments perceived necessary, there is no option to quit. Most of the time people get more and more bitter and say worse and worse things as the litigation proceeds. When this is over, the lawyers and judges go home, and you are left to deal and co-parent with the person you have just publicly maligned.

- If litigation looms, and your spouse has retained the shark with the reputation for removing body parts and coming at you no matter what, you should select counsel that will not engage in that type of fight. The fight is really what they feed on. There are many good lawyers who will stand firm and not rise to the bait of a bloodletting. Look around, and don't just hire the first lawyer you see; find someone who will understand your needs and minimize the animosity. The judge will appreciate that. Remember, judges probably already know the shark's tactics, and none approve of them.

Hon. W. Ross Foote (Ret.), Alexandria, Louisiana

Practical Aspects of Litigation

It's a widespread belief that in most cases, litigation offers the least satisfactory resolution. Not only is it the most expensive route to go, but you also have to give a judge—a third party, a stranger—the sole authority to determine what your life is going to look like (except in the few states in which divorce cases are heard by a jury). The court can only provide limited resolutions to certain problems, and many lawyers have told me that the court is not interested in many issues that might be important to you. You may feel that there is inequity when dividing up assets. You might think it's important that your children have access to tutoring and extracurricular programs—or to Cub Scouts and skiing, or to private school. But a judge will make those decisions—and, with the courts so overloaded with cases, you'll have little time to convince him or her of what you need. Sometimes the judge will not even have read the materials in advance.

A court has limited time, power, and procedural flexibility to resolve all of the problems you and your family face. Because of its limited time, it may make orders that do not attend to the details about which you are rightfully concerned. Because of its limited power, it will not generally concern itself with all of the affected family members in a blended family, just those who are part of the original family. Because it grows out of a system that was designed for criminal cases and other matters where there is right and wrong, guilty and innocent, it does not work well for families in crisis, where it is impossible (or not useful) to determine fault. It is a public forum being used for private concerns. It leads people to get set in hardened positions instead of addressing each other's needs. It provides not a way to listen, but, rather, a way to fight. I would go so far as to say it is generally a harmful way to resolve problems for those couples who will have an ongoing relationship as parents of their children.

Lawyer Fern Topas Salka, Fern Topas Salka, Los Angeles, California

Lawyers find it frustrating if a judge they are presenting to has little or no experience in family law. This is the case in many jurisdictions, and in many others, it is not. Lawyers look to the presiding judge to deliver judgment fairly without a bias, but judges do have their own value codes. Some judges have reputations for holding certain perspectives—for instance, they may be wife-minded or husband-minded. Judges are sensitive to custody situations and might order a custody and access assessment (this is outlined in chapter 8) to help them with these particular decisions. Judges react most negatively to a parent who makes false charges of physical or sexual abuse against the other parent.

You will have the most credibility before a judge if you are able to bring a balanced perception of what occurred in the marriage—if you can take responsibility for your own shortcomings and offer an appropriate critique of your spouse. In addition, you can't expect the judge to make great decisions if your case is not well prepped and you don't present the evidence you should. This is why you need to work with a highly skilled trial lawyer who knows how to prepare and present the case.

Judges are rational, thinking people who react best to the reasonable positions that stand the test of exposure. It is the "reasonable man" test, long used in other areas of the law. What would a reasonable person do under the circumstances?

Lawyer Armin Kuder, Kuder, Smoller & Friedman, Washington, D.C.

Be aware, however, that your lawyer can't control your spouse, who your spouse hires as a lawyer, or how they are going to litigate. Your lawyer cannot guarantee common sense from the other side. While your lawyer can try to keep costs down, sometimes you incur costs because of a lack of response from the opposing side, or because you're forced to respond to many letters from the other side in what becomes a "document war."

To be on top of the litigation process, you must be highly alert and react more from a business perspective than an emotional one, which certainly isn't easy. No one can predict what a judge or opposing lawyer is going to do, but you can minimize the chances of disaster by being as straightforward, honest, and reasonable as possible with your own lawyer.

Appeals

What happens when you lose in court and are not satisfied with the decision? You can appeal. *Appeal* means a request to have a panel of judges review any legal issues related to your case. Generally, an appeal will challenge the judge's legal interpretations, rather than his or her findings regarding the facts of the case; findings of fact are extremely difficult to appeal.

Under what circumstances would you most likely appeal?

- When the law clearly allowed the judge's decision to follow several different paths, and the path he or she chose was less favorable to your side.
- When the judge's decision includes an interpretation of an important issue of law that has not been previously deter-

mined in his or her jurisdiction (called *first impression* or, in Canada, *fresh impression*). If the ruling seems reasonable, however, an appeal on this basis is difficult, because you have to get over the hurdle of the judge's discretion.

- When there is so much money involved that it might be worth the expense of an appeal to try to get the amount of the judgment adjusted.
- When you have a slight chance of overturning the judgment, but the issue is so important to you that you feel it's worth a try (for instance, if you feel strongly about a child custody issue).

How much is custody worth to you? How much is protecting your child worth to you? How much is having more time with your child worth to you? Many of these things are invaluable. In custody cases, unless you have a pretty clear legal issue, as opposed to a factual issue, don't even think about appealing. Custody, like many issues in family law, is modifiable on changes of circumstances. I always want people to think about this: would you rather take your litigation fund and spend it all on an appeal, or would you rather save it and bring a later modification motion? One of the more difficult analyses, particularly in a custody case, in whether or not to appeal is whether there is some issue in the order that will haunt you for the rest of your case.

Appellate lawyer Paige Leslie Wickland,
Fancher & Wickland, San Francisco, California

Do you need a new lawyer to appeal? It's up to you. Some people switch lawyers because the original one could not settle and they remain angry about that. The dissatisfaction could be an outgrowth of the now-divorced person's own failure to negotiate or accept a reasonable outcome; some lawyers have said that the losing side will switch their warriors because of the same frustrations or imbalances that led them to trial in the first place.

Enforcement

The judicial system is honor based. Most people usually abide by the decision of the judge whether they agree with it or not. However, there are instances where people will not obey the ruling. The best way to ensure enforcement is with a court order that allows you to bring the defiant person back to court or to an arbitrator (and usually requires that person to pay your legal fees if you do). That's why separation agreements, settlement agreements, and final judgments of divorce are incorporated into a court order—so that if the agreement or ruling isn't obeyed, you can take action. Some lawyers would recommend that you always structure the final order to provide for arbitration rather than another round of court appearances.

If you anticipate that collecting child support or spousal support will be an issue, your lawyer can put you in contact with the government agency whose role is to make sure that support payments are collected and paid. This government office has the legal authority to take action against those that do not meet their family obligations.

Which Option Is Right for You?

Even choosing which dispute resolution option to take can become a fight for a divorcing couple. Don't invest yourself in particular outcomes. Your goal should be as reasonable a dissolution of your marriage as possible under the circumstances. You do not have—and you will not be able to get—complete control of the options or of how the other side acts within them.

A good lawyer will emphasize that it is extremely unlikely that anyone is going to walk away having won completely. I've been told by many lawyers that they make most of their money from clients who are stubborn. But many lawyers also say that they would accept slightly lower fees for easier clients, even if they have to take on more clients to make up the difference.

Lawyers ask clients a lot of questions to determine which ADR model is appropriate. Has there been any domestic violence? Have there been any special concerns? Are there any problems of substance abuse? Do they have any special needs with regard to their children? How much do they want to spend on the divorce? I'm trying to get the client to tell me, at the very beginning, what the expectations are, how he or she wants this divorce to end, and what the long-term goal is.

Lawyer Ronald Supancic, Family Law Offices of Ronald M. Supancic, Woodland Hills, California

---

Most lawyers know, within certain parameters, what the financial outcomes of most divorce cases will be, and that this outcome will be roughly the same no matter what form of resolution is used. The emotional impact of each process, though, is significantly different, and the cost of litigation can be so great that, after paying legal fees, you end up with nothing.

I experienced this firsthand. At one point during my long divorce, we went into mediation to determine child support payments. But one of us wouldn't sign the agreement, forcing us into litigation. The final outcome was, financially speaking, almost the same as it would have been had we successfully mediated. But the cost to get there was thousands of dollars more. From an emotional perspective the experience was exasperating, and our relationship deteriorated significantly.

The total cost, like the amount of time it may to take to complete your divorce, is difficult to predict. The nature and extent of the assets, the complexity of the legal issues, and the cooperation of the parties are significant factors.

Lawyer David M. Wildstein, Wilentz,
Goldman & Spitzer, PA, Woodbridge, New Jersey

Lawyers are obliged to explain the different modalities available to arrive at resolution. Negotiation takes place in all of them. The best result is one in which there is full disclosure of assets and liabilities, where there are some options, and where the relationship between the two adults, when there are children, can be reconfigured from one of former intimate partners to that of co-parents.

Lawyer Carren S. Oler, Law Office of Carren S. Oler, Rockville, Maryland

An interesting way of describing how you can evaluate your legal options was explained this way by many lawyers: Imagine yourself five years from now—what do you want your relationship with your former spouse to look like? Do you want joint birthday parties? Do you see yourself calling your ex and saying, "Johnny wants a tattoo—what do you think?" Or do you want to have nothing to do with your ex-spouse? Examine in your own heart what you want your life to look like. Then think about the type of process that will give you this result. That is how to decide. For example, negotiation, mediation, or collaborative law will more likely result in an ongoing, amicable relationship with your ex than would litigation.

Some people have no clue what they want their lives to be like past the divorce, and that's perfectly fine. Other people give you very detailed descriptions. The people who don't have a clue are the ones who need to become focused on planning. A lawyer can't get proper instruction from clients unless they have some goals in mind and unless they are looking forward.

Lawyer Jim Stoffman, Taylor McCaffrey, Winnipeg, Manitoba

5

Finding Your Legal Eagle

My head was spinning. I wasn't sure where to turn, where to start, or what to ask. I did not take control. I did not do my own due diligence—fact finding—when I went in search of a lawyer.

What I should have done was to take a big breath, research my options, and start my divorce with confidence. I realized many years, tens of thousands of dollars, and three lawyers later why it is so important to find the right lawyer: because whoever you choose is going to help you make decisions about your money, future, and children—concerns that are so important to you and your family.

Choosing the right lawyer may be your most important decision in ending your marriage and successfully beginning the next phase of your life. The right matrimonial lawyer can help provide you with financial security. The wrong lawyer may lead to the loss of marital assets that are rightfully yours, or even may result in your losing custody of your children. Your lawyer should be part of your solution, not part of your problem. You owe it to yourself to choose carefully and to choose the best lawyer for you.

Lawyer David M. Wildstein, Wilentz,
Goldman & Spitzer, PA, Woodbridge, New Jersey

In order to have confidence in the decisions you make, you have to trust, respect, and have confidence in the lawyer you hire. Make sure this person is reputable, capable, and skilled.

As a good divorce lawyer, you have to be able to be empathetic and understanding. Many divorce lawyers are not, and the person hiring that divorce lawyer has to understand that. What type of lawyer is it? Is it somebody who is going to pat you on the head and say, "Yes, dear" or "Yes, sir"? Is it a collaborative-type lawyer? Is it a partnership-type lawyer? Is it somebody who's a screamer? Is it somebody who litigates everything? Is it somebody who doesn't know his or her way around a courtroom and can only settle things?

Lawyer Stacy D. Phillips, Phillips, Lerner,
Lauzon & Jamra, Los Angeles, California

This is not a job; this is a life. We are entrusted with a client's and this society's most sacred mission. You can destroy a family with the wrong moves.

Lawyer Glenn C. Lewis, Lewis Law Firm, Washington, D.C.

You and your spouse should retain separate legal counsel. It would be a conflict of interest for a lawyer to represent both of you. After all, whose side would the lawyer best represent?

Build a List of Possible Lawyers

To begin your search, make a list of lawyers in your area and within your budget considerations who specialize in family law— not those who dabble in family law, or those who specialize in other areas but would take your case as a favor to you. Retaining a family law lawyer is critical. In addition, bar associations and law societies in many jurisdictions offer additional certification to lawyers who demonstrate their ability in a particular specialty—a lawyer who has proven his ability in family law is known as a *certified family law specialist*. Certification, or lack thereof, is not a conclusive measure of ability, but it is another factor worth considering as you compile your list of lawyers.

Here are some ways to generate your list:

- Other lawyers or professionals who have regular contact with matrimonial lawyers can provide referrals.
- Numerous legal Web sites provide lawyer referrals (see "Resources," page 184, for a partial list of such sites).
- Your therapist or another mental health professional can recommend lawyers.
- Others who have gone through divorce can direct you to the lawyers they used. Also ask these people who represented their former spouses, and who they thought was the better lawyer.

One way to locate a good lawyer is to go to a firm that has a quality reputation and look for some of the younger lawyers in that firm whose hourly rates may be lower and more appropriate to your needs, but who are still supervised by someone more senior in the firm who has a superb and well-known reputation.

Lawyer Sanford K. Ain, Ain & Bank, Washington, D.C.

The best way to look for a lawyer is to go to one of the accredited organizations, get some names of people, and cross-check them against a list of lawyers your friends have used and liked. Friends can't be your only method of determining who is good; they could be raving about somebody who was right for them and right for their case, but who will not necessarily be right for your case. Any lawyer you consider should have some basic accreditation. That doesn't ensure that he or she is a great lawyer, and that doesn't mean that the lawyer will be good for you. See if the lawyer you're considering has a disciplinary record. This is a good way to do your cross-checking.

Lawyer Peter M. Walzer, Walzer & Melcher, LLP, Beverly Hills, California

---

Once you have your list of lawyers, you need to narrow down that list. Research the lawyers on the Internet or ask around to find out more information about them. Think about how you would like your future to look, and pick several lawyers from the list whom you think can help you to achieve those goals. Set up a *consultation*, or meeting, with each of them. You should consider speaking to at least three lawyers, because different lawyers will have different strategies and plans that can be equally valid.

The Consultation

Setting up a meeting or consultation with a prospective lawyer is an excellent way to determine if he or she is right for you. Some lawyers refer to the search for the right lawyer as the "beauty contest." However, this is not the time to pick a lawyer who could win an award for Mr. or Ms. Congeniality or who has the best wardrobe or the prettiest office. It's very important to go beyond the facade.

On some level, your consultation is just a pretense for being with the person long enough to know whether you feel comfortable with him or her. Many of the lawyers who discussed this topic with me agreed that for the relationship to work best, there should be "chemistry"—a good personality fit. They stated how important it is that both parties feel at ease.

A person should, first of all, ensure that the lawyer is confident. And the next thing is chemistry, how you feel with that person. That's very important, because you are going to be spending a lot of time with him or her. Third, what attitudes does the lawyer have toward the case? What does the lawyer think is an appropriate or fair resolution of the case? If another lawyer is going to be involved in the case, you need to meet that person as well. You have to meet the team.

Lawyer Harold Niman, Niman Zemans Gelgoot, Toronto, Ontario

There are three things you need to keep a marriage intact—truth, communication, and compromise—and these are the same three things that you need when you want to come to a separation agreement. You need to be able to communicate with a lawyer accurately and impartially, and there has to be trust in terms of the advice that you're getting. You have to be prepared to approach the settlement with a degree of compromise. You then have to sort out your needs versus your wants. You need to be prepared to listen; you need to have a lawyer who's going to tell you what you need to hear as opposed to what you want to hear. And you have to set aside all those frustrated notions of your own entitlement and accept what the law provides.

Lawyer Jim Stoffman, Taylor McCaffrey, Winnipeg, Manitoba

Just as every client has a different personality, lawyers have different skill sets and styles that need to be considered. There are lawyers who have expertise in certain areas, such as estate planning, financial issues, or child-related issues. Lawyers also have varying philosophies. There are feminist lawyers, collaborative practice lawyers, trial lawyers, and so on. With so many factors to consider, the consultation process should not be undertaken lightly. You must go into each meeting thinking of it as a highly sophisticated business transaction. Keep in mind that as you assess the lawyer to determine whether he or she is a good fit, the lawyer is also assessing you.

Consider bringing along a friend or family member around whom you are comfortable discussing the initial details of your separation. If you are in an emotional state, it's likely that you won't fully hear or properly process the lawyer's initial advice. A friend may help calm your emotions and can serve as a backup set of ears at the meeting. However, you should carefully weigh whom to bring. You never know what is going to come out during a consultation, and some information may not be appropriate for a friend or family member to know. You don't want to end up withholding important information because there's someone else in the room.

There are really a couple of ways of doing consultations. One way is the "let's meet each other" kind of consultation. We're not going to be talking about your case; what we are going to be doing is just getting to know each other to see whether we are a good fit. That's generally a much briefer conversation. You want to know my credentials, you want to test my personality and just see what I think of the world. That would be one way of doing it.

There is also a working consultation. I ask people to bring in enough information so that, whether they hire me or they don't hire me, they can walk away with sufficient information to be well armed, in terms of knowledge, to go forward. What do you bring to the consultation? Bring in financial information so that we can, in the very first meeting, not only get to know each other but talk about the gross parameters of your case, so that I'm not wasting time talking about issues that are not relevant. I get some information about what issues are relevant to you, and then we talk about the ways that they can be addressed. We also talk about processes—which are appropriate for your case and which might not be appropriate.

Lawyer Dianna Gould-Saltman, Gould-Saltman
Law Offices, LLP, Los Angeles, California

Don't make a commitment to hire a lawyer during the consultation, for two reasons:

1. Chances are, if you share a significant amount of information with the prospective lawyer at the consultation, you'll be exhausted and will be processing a lot of new information. You will most likely be able to think more clearly once you're sitting at home, or after talking it over with a trusted friend or relative.

2. As a prospective client, you cannot judge whether the lawyer will do a good job of pleading your case or if he or she can draft documents properly. What you can determine is simply this: *do I like the sound of how he or she presents?* You need time to think about this question after your meeting, and to compare his or her presentation skills to those of other lawyers.

What to Ask

Make the meeting work for you by being prepared with questions such as the following:

- Are you a family law lawyer, and are you certified as a family law specialist?
- How many years have you been practicing family law?
- What is your belief in regard to the family and the role of the lawyer?

- What are my legal rights and obligations?
- Do you believe the allegations coming from each side? Will you investigate them?
- What will my role and responsibilities be in helping to move through my divorce?
- What is your hourly rate? How do the billings and retainers work?
- How do you prefer that your client communicate with you? E-mail, teleconference, or personal meetings?
- What is your usual response time for returning phone calls?
- Will I approve letters before they go out, and will you copy me on all letters going in and out?
- Do you have the time for my case?
- What is your approach to settling a case? Do you have a preferred approach to dispute resolution? How often do you go to court, and how often does this end in a trial (a decision made by a judge)?
- How do you settle cases and what is the process?
- Have you handled a case like mine before and had similar issues? How did you handle it? Do you handle complex issues and how do you deal with them?
- What strategy do you recommend I follow for financial issues? For child-related issues? Do we deal with each separately or at the same time, and why?
- Do you delegate tasks to other individuals or do you do everything yourself?
- Can I meet other members of your team?
- Under what circumstances would you advocate bringing in nonlawyers (for instance, family counselors) to offer their expertise on the issues of the case?
- What other professionals do you typically deal with and who are they?

- What experience do you have dealing with personality disorder issues, or mental or physical abuse? (Ask this only if it's relevant to your own divorce.)
- Are you teaching in the profession?
- Have you published any articles related to family law, and if so, where did these appear?
- Do you have a recommended reading list or handouts?
- Have you ever been disciplined or disbarred by a bar association?
- Have you or your insurance company paid on any malpractice claims?
- Do you carry malpractice insurance?

Listen carefully to the lawyer's responses, and take notes. Try to evaluate his or her attitudes and procedures.

Talk philosophy. Every lawyer can talk about the nuts and bolts of a divorce, but it's vitally important for the client to make sure there is a synergy and rapport with the lawyer. For example, say the client wants to have a divorce in which there's not a lot of litigation, in which there's mutual respect, and in which the parties can have a civil relationship after the case—especially when there are children, so the parents can both attend weddings and other family events for their kids after the divorce and be civil, and everybody can feel comfortable. It's important to find a lawyer whose philosophy matches that outlook. It is perfectly OK to ask the lawyer, "What is your philosophy concerning settling cases? What is your philosophy regarding mediation and ADR?" Some clients are very detail-oriented and want a lawyer who fits that mode. Other clients want the big picture. They want a strategist. What I tell my divorce clients to help prepare them is to recognize that they are processing a lot of the information through emotion rather than through cognitive reasoning. It's OK to ask those questions. It's OK to ask whether the lawyer represents primarily men or women or whether the lawyer has any personal biases. It's all right to interview the lawyer. A good lawyer will not be upset by good, probing questions.

Lawyer Edward L. Winer, Moss & Barnett, Minneapolis, Minnesota

---

What to Watch Out For

Your listening and evaluation skills are critical for assessing whether a lawyer is right for you or whether you should cut your losses and move on to the next. Warning bells should go off if the lawyer promises you the world, because that's not usually something he or she can achieve. Some lawyers will say anything to retain a client; you need to do your own reality check.

If you are going to retain a lawyer, you have to have a sense of confidence in this lawyer. If you do not, you are then fighting your own lawyer as well as fighting the opposition. So it is kind of a gut check. You have a right to anticipate how the process is going to work. I think if a client hears a lawyer say, "You should get this and you should get that," "You should get twenty thousand dollars a month in alimony," or other things that pander to the client's fantasies, that should be a warning sign. If the client is hearing everything he or she wants to hear, then there is something wrong.

Lawyer Carole S. Gailor, Gailor, Wallis & Hunt, PLLC, Raleigh, North Carolina

---

In general, people feel very confident that their own financial information is accurate and that a lawyer should take it at face value. But a competent lawyer will want to confirm this information. People often walk into a lawyer's office and ask, "What am

I going to get?" If a lawyer gives you an answer before doing any fact checking, be wary. This lawyer isn't basing his or her opinion on solid data, and you could be disappointed later on if the results are not what was promised initially.

Often I can't tell clients what they will get because I don't have enough information. The kind of information I need is information that's got to be developed. I don't know what the business is worth. "Oh, it's worth millions," says the client. Well, yes, it may be, but I've got to have an expert who will tell the court and me what it is worth, so that I can appropriately advise you of what you are entitled to. And I can't tell you what you are entitled to until I have that information.

Lawyer Jack A. Rounick, Flamm, Boroff & Bacine, PC, Blue Bell, Pennsylvania

---

Your lawyer should not hesitate to answer your questions about fees. You can ask and should be told how much is expected up front in retainer fees, as well as the hourly rates of all the individuals who will be involved in your case.

Client expectations are managed by not promising more than you can deliver, especially at the initial meeting. Clients will not remember much about what you say to them regarding the law, or about the guidance you provide. However, they always remember the promises and predictions— how much it's going to cost, and what you are going to get for them. So you always want to provide answers that pretty much match how you think the case is going to come out—or slightly on the conservative side, because you cannot control all the variables out there. And if appropriate, you tell clients: "I may have a difficult time controlling you. I have no ability to control your spouse, your spouse's lawyer, the court, the experts, or the witnesses. It is very difficult to make predictions or promises with certainty. However, my best estimate would be that you are going to end up somewhere between x and y." The prudent lawyer puts it in writing and says periodically, "I may amend these predictions in either direction, but you asked me for my best estimates as of today regarding outcome, time to completion, legal fees, etc., and here they are, recognizing that these are just estimates."

Lawyer Allan R. Koritzinsky, Foley & Lardner, LLP, Madison, Wisconsin

Be sure to discuss any special procedures, such as financial investigations, you're interested in pursuing, to find out whether they'll cause you to incur additional costs.

We have clients who come in and say, "I want a forensic audit of my husband's business. I think there's a million dollars there. He says there's no money there. I want lawyers, I want accountants, I want this, I want that." And I may say, "Great, I'm happy to do all of that, but here's what you're looking at in terms of costs. Are you able to finance that?" People say money's not an object, and I say, "Let's talk about the real world here." And, you know, there are some people that are prepared to pay for it—they are saying the right things—but they just can't afford this. I say, "I'm not going to let you do that, because a year from now we're going to have an unhappy relationship." When someone is making forty thousand dollars a year and wants to commit to a process that's going to cost fifty thousand dollars—that is crazy. I always talk about money in the initial interviews so that people know what they are getting into. We have signed retainer agreements that clearly lay out our hourly rates for me, my juniors, and my staff, because the biggest problems between family law lawyers and their clients arise when lawyers do not dampen their client's unrealistic expectations and when lawyers are not clear enough about costs.

Lawyer Lorne Wolfson, Torkin Manes, Toronto, Ontario

The Decision

Armed with everything you've learned during the consultation process, you will most likely choose the right lawyer—if you really take the time to analyze the information you've gathered. I have heard people say they want someone who is a real barracuda, or someone who is litigious, or moderate. Think about what these things mean and what you actually want. If you are not a barracuda, you're not going to feel comfortable swimming in the same waters with one. A lawyer can be strong without being a barracuda.

Your lawyer can tell you your options and rights and give you support, but you have to make every decision. You have to pick a lawyer that you are able to work with for the long haul. You're not going to be able to do that if you're with someone you don't quite understand or feel comfortable with, or if you're worried that he or she doesn't like you because you're making "the wrong decisions."

A litigious lawyer is one who wants to try a case. Someone whose aptitudes and desire are to put you in a place of conflict rather than to make a good settlement. Someone who wants to be in front of a judge with your family. That is a litigious person. Anyone who would knowingly go to a litigious person . . . that's insane! That said, you need a lawyer who is willing to fight, who is highly skilled at trying a case, to protect yourself.

Lawyer Glenn C. Lewis, Lewis Law Firm, Washington, D.C.

Clients don't have to like their lawyer, but they do need to respect him or her. In the first interview with a client, I make it clear that if a client does not want to follow my advice, he or she should seek other counsel. Clients of moderate means speak with their friends at the book club and believe they are going to receive the same financial settlement that a friend who was married to a spouse worth hundreds of millions of dollars received, and that is not the case. If a client wants to run his or her case, the choice for counsel should be a lawyer that will permit the client to do whatever he or she wants. But that client is making a serious economic mistake, because chances are, the client's judgment is impaired by the current emotional and economic instability caused by divorce.

Lawyer Judith E. Siegel-Baum, Wolf, Block,
Schorr and Solis-Cohen, LLP, New York, New York

Here are some things to consider when making your decision:

- Does this lawyer seem confident, strong, and experienced?
- What skills do I see in this person? Is the lawyer smart, resourceful, comforting, strategic, a good listener, and so forth?
- Is this person a skilled negotiator, trial lawyer, and communicator?
- What kind of dispute resolution do I want to pursue, and does this lawyer have the appropriate experience and skills to handle the case in this fashion?
- How will the parenting plan be developed (if required)? Who will develop it?
- If there are realistic issues involving personality disorders, substance abuse, or other such problems, does the lawyer have the experience and skill set to deal effectively with them?
- Do I trust and respect this person? Can we have a good working partnership?
- Can I be honest with this person? Do I feel comfortable sharing intimate details?

- Is this person honest and candid with me?
- Does the lawyer pay attention to me? Does he or she have time for me?
- Can I afford this lawyer?

Does the lawyer want to *win* for you? This may be difficult to determine during an initial interview. However, there is a greater likelihood that the lawyer will be committed to your case if he or she is interested in your case. A lawyer's interest in your case may be revealed by a lively and energetic search for facts and detail.

Every case requires a plan of action consistent with goals that the lawyer and client mutually agree upon. Unless your lawyer develops a strategy and remains focused on your goals, your case may become prolonged and costly. During the interview, ask the lawyer what result could be reasonably obtained and what strategies could be implemented to achieve your goals. The lawyer's response to this question will give you insight into his or her analytical skills and ability to develop a blueprint.

Make sure you choose a lawyer who is willing and able to adapt to your changing needs. Though you may want a lawyer who is sensitive and compassionate toward you, keep in mind that these qualities alone are insufficient. There are also times when your lawyer must be assertive and tenacious, especially when dealing with your spouse, your spouse's lawyer, and the court. A lawyer who exudes strength and confidence during your initial interview is more likely to be able to be aggressive when the need arises.

Lawyer David M. Wildstein, Wilentz,
Goldman & Spitzer, PA, Woodbridge, New Jersey

Big Firm or Small Firm: Finding the Right Fit

Should you seek out a big firm? How about a small boutique firm specializing in family law instead? How do you know which to hire? There are many factors to consider. If you have a large, complex estate with significant business, tax, or real estate issues that could complicate asset and custody decisions, you need to select a firm that has lawyers with the right experiences to handle these issues. For example, if a family business or significant voting stock is at stake, you might want your lawyer to have the ability to consult with a family business law practitioner.

Big Firm

In complex cases, make sure that the firm has a trust and estate lawyer, a real estate lawyer, a pension person, and a tax person on hand, because you would not want to have your lawyer go to outside people to do the job that may need to be done on your behalf. You would like to keep it all in one place to minimize economic drain. It's a good idea to hire a firm that has all these supporting lawyers.

Lawyer Judith E. Siegel-Baum, Wolf, Block,
Schorr and Solis-Cohen, LLP, New York, New York

On the other hand, boutique family law firms offer their own advantages. Because these firms handle only family law cases, this aspect of the law is their particular area of expertise.

Small Firm

Divorce is no longer a by-product of a big law firm, and you don't want to go to a big civil firm and have their one divorce lawyer do your divorce. The way to get your divorce now, whatever economic strata you come from, is to go to a divorce specialty firm.

Lawyer Mike McCurley, McCurley Orsinger
McCurley Nelson & Downing, LLP, Dallas, Texas

What if You Made a Bad Choice?

Switching lawyers takes time and costs a lot of money, and in family law, it is not unusual for clients to misuse this option. They may go from lawyer to lawyer until they find one that tells them what they want to hear. That doesn't mean that that lawyer is a better lawyer, it doesn't change reality, and it doesn't mean that they're going to get a better deal. Some people switch lawyers because they don't understand what they should expect in the first place; they have very unrealistic goals, and when their lawyer doesn't achieve them, they find another one.

However, any one lawyer, no matter how good he or she is, is not right for everyone. Remember, you are the boss. You need to feel comfortable with the process, the strategy, and the agreement you may ultimately be asked to sign. You do not want to regret decisions you have made. If you are unsure about any part of the process, get a second opinion from another lawyer. (If you are unsure about an agreement you are about to sign, get a second opinion before you sign, not after. If you wait until after it's signed to change your mind, you have already made a legal commitment, and you can't get out of it easily without spending a large amount of money to try to correct your mistake, if indeed you can.)

You are in charge of your case. Change lawyers if you feel uncomfortable. If necessary, find a new lawyer before dropping the one you have, just in case you decide not to change. Sometimes potential clients meet with a new lawyer to discuss dissatisfactions with their current lawyer. After a brief discussion, they often realize that their lawyer is actually doing a good job under the circumstances. It is better not to change lawyers frequently. It tends to give the impression that you are a difficult personality, and that may negatively affect your case in the eyes of the court.

Mediator and lawyer William A. Eddy, National
Conflict Resolution Center, San Diego, California

If you decide you do need to change lawyers, be aware it is more strategically advantageous to do so at certain times than at others.

If you're thinking about switching lawyers, do it at a strategic time that's best for you. If you're awaiting a questioning, discovery, or deposition, try to find fresh counsel before that procedure takes place. Don't have your current lawyer do that if you're having second thoughts about him or her. Jump ship and get somebody else up to speed, because that questioning, discovery, or deposition is the record you will be stuck with.

Lawyer Nicole Tellier, Nicole Tellier Law Offices, Toronto, Ontario

---

The process of finding the right lawyer can be exhausting, but empowering at the same time. Of course, the real work is yet to come. Once the choice is made, you need to know how to work effectively with your legal counsel to continue your quest for a smart divorce.

6

Working Effectively with Your Lawyer

Asmart divorce involves moving effectively through the divorce process and understanding the roles both you and your lawyer play during this time. Although you're the one paying for the lawyer's services, you must be involved and realize it's a job for you, too. This chapter explores the roles of both lawyer and client and outlines some strategies for working effectively together in order to save you time and money.

Your Lawyer's Job

Develop Realistic Expectations

One of the first things you will do with your lawyer is to discuss what you can expect to receive or pay out in terms of spousal support, child support, custody of and access to the children, and division of matrimonial assets. Each jurisdiction has its own divorce guidelines, so it is up to your lawyer to advise you of the rights, rules, obligations, and entitlements that apply to your particular case.

Oftentimes people think that they are entitled to get, or will have to pay, a certain amount because they heard about someone somewhere who got, or paid, exactly that. Sometimes people are angry and want their former partners to "pay" for their divorce. I've heard many people who are going through divorce say, "She's not going to get a dime out of me," or "I'm going to make him pay for this." It just doesn't happen like that, and your lawyer should make this clear.

A good divorce lawyer should start the process of working on those unreasonable expectations early on. If you don't know anything about this area of this law, on what basis do you set your expectations? The truth is that divorce hurts lots of people, and divorce hurts lots of children. It doesn't need to be as bad as it is. It does not have to be the catastrophe that it oftentimes is. And a big part of that responsibility is in the hands and the lap of the divorce lawyer in charge.

Lawyer Mike McCurley, McCurley Orsinger
McCurley Nelson & Downing, LLP, Dallas, Texas

If a lawyer permits a client to have unrealistic expectations, the process ends only in disappointment.

You have to tell clients the truth: "If you think you're going to hurt him, think again; that's not going to happen." They must be given correct information about what is going to occur. Sometimes what the client wants is so extreme, I won't represent them. If they want me to do things that are inappropriate or unethical, I just won't do it. And they go out and get somebody else, and eventually they've wasted a lot of money in lawyer's fees and destroyed themselves and their kids. I try to give them the big picture of what's going to happen in their divorce and what the process is. Then I emphasize talking with the therapist they've been seeing to give them some insight into their behavior and unrealistic expectations.

Lawyer Nicholas A. Leto Jr., Veltmann & Leto, LLP, San Diego, California

Maximize the Economic Outcome

Lawyers view their job as getting the best deals for their clients, but the best deal may not necessarily be the biggest number, because there are other issues as well. Sometimes a lawyer prefers a smaller deal to ensure that the client will collect what was agreed to be paid, or to avoid a trial that might further damage the relationship between parties who must continue to co-parent their children. For this reason, a lawyer's idea of the best deal and the client's idea of the best deal may be different, and sometimes lawyers must get clients to realize that what is best for them isn't necessarily what they *think* is best.

Really, the lawyer's job is to ensure economic security. However, if clients are not careful and alert to this, they will spend more money and compromise their economic security. They spend so much money on fighting and create such an adversarial climate with their partner that they will fight for the rest of their lives and will never really have any money. What it requires is recognition that this is a business deal.

Lawyer Jeffery Wilson, Wilson Christen, LLP, Toronto, Ontario

Look Out for Your Children's Best Interests

Many lawyers' first focus with their clients is on working things out for the children. Unfortunately, some parents are still so emotionally distraught, or were such poor parents in the first place, that they do things that are in their own best interests, not the children's. They attempt to hurt the other parent, which is ultimately bad for the children. Ethical lawyers will not deal with crazy agendas and destructive goals.

How can I help a client if I don't service the needs of the children first? What is the most important thing in life? Raising children—for society, for ourselves, for our values, for our morals, religion, ethics—however you wish to describe it. Children are the ones without a voice—unless someone gives them a voice. I strap it on my client, proudly: We're looking out for the kids. Therefore, isn't it in your best interests to produce a good outcome for the children? And won't a child eventually resent the parent who assists in marginalizing his or her relationship with the other parent? Therefore, it follows that my client's interests are well served by treating all concerned with at least some modicum of respect. Say an aggressive guy (or woman; this is a gender-neutral proposition) walks in and demands that the opponent be treated rudely, or in a manner somehow inappropriately. I would never do that gratuitously. Instead—and this actually *is* in his best interests and is a way, I hope, to begin training him for his lifetime role as a co-parent—I ask him, "How is it in my client's interest to destroy his children's mother? It never can be. All children are well served by having an intact mother."

Lawyer Glenn C. Lewis, Lewis Law Firm, Washington, D.C.

Your Lawyer's Roles

In order for a lawyer to fulfill the responsibilities outlined above, he or she must play various roles.

Ringmaster

To get you through this difficult time, your lawyer is responsible for running many shows at once: educating you on right versus wrong; providing you with a reality check; listening; assessing your goals; and helping you to achieve a reasonable and fair settlement—one you can live with and won't complain about for years to come.

Your lawyer also has to know when to enlist others to assist with his or her many responsibilities—and who those assistants should be. Many lawyers' firms have support staff or junior lawyers who, with the client's approval, can handle certain aspects of the case more cost-effectively. Lawyers will also call on experts in specific areas such as budgeting, accounting, and parenting as needed.

For example, when the case gets complicated and requires much financial analysis—say, if you need to determine the value of your spouse's business—your lawyer will bring in a forensic accounting expert to help. For other issues, the lawyer may rely on parenting experts. A client may feel that his or her own expert—for instance, a personal accountant—could do the job, but divorce requires a different kind of accounting expertise. The client has to understand that the lawyer is not doing it to run up the bill—that, in fact, in the long run it's going to benefit the client.

Counselor

At the beginning of the divorce process, some lawyers take things slowly, step by step. It is hard to do everything right away because of the emotional state of most clients—they tend to say or do things that could be detrimental to their cases. Be careful; everything you say and everything you write (in any form, including letters, e-mails, and so on) can be used against you. A good lawyer will counsel you on how to deal with your emotional state so that you can make good decisions. (In some jurisdictions, he or she may even be required by law to discuss whether there's a possibility that you and your spouse will reconcile.)

The lawyer's most important role is to help the client recognize the emotions that he or she is going through, to educate the client to make good decisions, and to promote as quick a settlement as reasonably possible in order to avoid the financial and emotional expense of unnecessary litigation. The role is basically to help the client put his or her life back together. I tell clients, "Your entire world has been pulled out from under you—relationships with friends, everything. There are many parts of that world that defined you as a couple—friends, family, the other person's family, religious places you go to, your jobs. Everything is kind of hybridized together. You have to unravel that big ball of twine and then put it back together in a different way, with a big part of it missing."

Mediator and lawyer William A. Eddy, National Conflict
Resolution Center, San Diego, California

My belief is that the client should be treated as an adult, not patronized, and should be as involved as he or she is capable of being and wants to be. The client should be fully informed as to what the process is, why the process is, and why the recommendations that are made are made.

What we do is set up a team. We have the supervising lawyer—which is the senior partner or another partner—a paralegal, and a client. The client always has someone to talk to. No question is too dumb. If my sense is that the client is still in a state of denial, grief, shock, I urge and occasionally insist that he or she get counseling, because I can't be his or her psychological counselor.

We ask clients to participate in the work, such as getting the background information for financial affidavits. I think that is more cost-effective for the clients; they feel a real connection to what is happening, and they're given some control over their own situations. I encourage them to participate in the process so that the whole thing is not such a mystery, and so they don't feel acted upon. And finally, I show them that I care, and I do.

Lawyer Carole S. Gailor, Gailor, Wallis & Hunt, PLLC, Raleigh, North Carolina

---

Some lawyers argue that it's important that their clients not use them as a substitute for an actual therapist. If you want to use your lawyer most effectively, you need to consider what his or her expertise really is—legal counsel—and use other professionals where appropriate in order to minimize your legal costs.

Lawyers are not licensed to provide therapy or counseling services. But lawyers need to be sensitive to the more personal concerns of a client, be patient, and direct the client to an appropriate professional.

Lawyer Mark S. Patt, Trope and Trope, Los Angeles, California

---

Conversely, lawyer Glenn C. Lewis, of the Lewis Law Firm in Washington, D.C., comments that he has to know mental health as well as a therapist does. "I'd never look at a client and say, 'Stop there. I will not discuss that; I am not your therapist.' Clients should steer clear of any lawyer who so starkly shuts down such a cry for help. What some may call venting, I consider an opportunity to gather critical facts." Lewis goes on to say, "If I don't listen to that three to five hours of venting, my client may suffer a 50 percent increased likelihood of losing everything they've ever cared about. Besides, clients are so grateful for such sessions. After listening to their concerns, a therapist might say, 'What do you think?' With me, albeit at a much higher hourly rate, I may actually give them answers! The lawyer can give a client practical solutions to problems he or she is concerned about, all the while improving that client's legal position. So, it's one-stop shopping, with the client's stress reduced, the client's confidence increased, and the client's outcome enhanced!"

Strategist and Moral Compass

My lawyer always took the high ground. I remember one occasion when there were false allegations coming from the other side, and I was outraged. I tried to hit back and told my lawyer a story. My lawyer looked directly in my eyes and asked, "Is this really true?" With my eyes averted and looking down, I quietly said, "No, but how come the other side can do it?" My lawyer understood my frustration, but protected me from getting caught up in it.

When it comes to self-centered and vindictive behavior, lawyers have different strategies to help their clients see the negative consequences. Glenn Lewis "takes out the baseball bat." It's a metaphor, he says, "but the point is that some clients walk in wrong-minded, every day seemingly wanting to do something terribly self-destructive or destructive of the family. That's when I take the baseball bat out and 'gently' pummel them behind closed doors, safely, where it is confidential and no one will ever know the truth about what they were about to do."

Mary H. Wechsler, of Wechsler Becker, LLP, in Seattle, Washington, helps her clients look at their actions in terms of "how the court or a mental health professional would look at it. I don't want to come across making moral judgments about my clients. When clients do something that does not appear to be focused on their children's needs, or that could be harmful to the children, I say, 'I know how you feel, but if the court were going to look at this situation, or if a parenting evaluator were going to look at this situation, they would see this behavior as harmful to the children.'" Wechsler helps clients to reframe their thinking. "It helps their case if they are good parents. So, if I see evidence of bad parenting or an inability to focus on the children, I always say something. Obviously, there are ethics for lawyers and divorces. If lawyers are uncomfortable with the ethics of their clients, they sometimes must withdraw."

I have certain rules. Many times clients will say, "He or she lied; the other lawyer lied; why can't we?" I will not lie or let my client lie, at least to my knowledge; that is in my retainer agreement. If my client is going way overboard, in a way that prevents me from supporting his or her position, then I will fire that client. If I find out clients have lied, or want to lie, I will also fire them. They don't have to do what I want them to do, because it is their lives, but they must be honest and within the realm of reason. And, if it's something I can't stand behind, especially when it comes to children, I won't be a part of it.

Lawyer Stacy D. Phillips, Phillips, Lerner,
Lauzon & Jamra, Los Angeles, California

Educator and Listener

A smart divorce is all about understanding and education. The lawyer's role is to facilitate your understanding.

In order to help with the education process, Dianna Gould-Saltman, of Gould-Saltman Law Offices, LLP, in Los Angeles, California, wants to ensure that her clients have their facts straight. She asks them, "What do you mean by that?" She wants to understand exactly what they are thinking, because oftentimes clients use words that they've heard somewhere—either on television or from their neighbor, or from one of a few other lawyers they've talked with—with no real understanding of their meaning. Gould-Saltman says she assesses "not only their level of intellectual understanding, but also their realistic expectations of the process. . . . I like them to understand the law. I want them to have a basic level of understanding of what the words and phrases mean, particularly because family law varies from state to state. So we need to make sure we are all talking the same language and that we have the same understanding of what the limits of the law are."

Information is power; education is everything. The goal in this case is for me to educate you to the max, and for you to educate me to the max. You're walking in with 100 percent of the information about the family. I'm walking in with 100 percent of the information about the system, the law, and all available options. So, I'll train you, you'll train me, and it's beautiful.

Lawyer Glenn C. Lewis, Lewis Law Firm, Washington, D.C.

You must gain your clients' confidence that you are hearing them, that you recognize their concerns, that you accept their goals as being reasonable, and that you are suggesting a mechanism that will result in an efficient use of their time and money.

Cheryl Lynn Hepfer, Law Offices of Cheryl Lynn Hepfer, Rockville, Maryland

---

Don't be afraid to ask questions if you need clarification about something. Don't leave the office if you really don't understand. Your lawyer is the expert and should provide you with this education.

Reality Coach

Your lawyer must be honest with you, which is not necessarily consistent with telling you what you may want to hear. Earlier in this chapter I discussed managing expectations. Your legal eagle can help you distinguish what is realistic and achievable from what is unrealistic or impossible.

I am conservative in expressing what can be expected. I make it a point never to raise expectations beyond that which is reasonably attainable. Keeping clients from going "off the deep end" with their expectations is very important.

Lawyer Stephen A. Kolodny, Kolodny & Anteau, Beverly Hills, California

---

Analyst and Adviser

Lawyers, by virtue of their training, are taught to take positions, analyze, and solve problems. These skills translate into helping you evaluate whether certain legal battles are worth fighting and what the relevant cost is, both emotionally and financially. This is called the *cost-benefit analysis*. Most lawyers will analyze your options in this way and advise you as to whether or not you should pursue them—but they will not decide for you. This is where the role of educator overlaps with that of adviser and analyst.

The lawyer's job can be complex, and every lawyer does things differently. You need to feel comfortable with the way yours does his or her job. Now, onto *your* job.

It's a Job for You, Too

Treat your divorce like a job. How is this done? By being organized, having realistic expectations, doing whatever work you can do yourself in a timely way, taking responsibility, and accessing as much information as possible. There is a lot to do. But don't let it take over your life and be all consuming.

Working with your lawyer is a balancing act. You need to be involved in your divorce proceedings, but not to manage them.

You have to make sure that you do your homework and that the bill gets paid. But if you attempt to run the case yourself, many lawyers caution, it will most certainly go awry.

It is the emotional and educational preparation that takes the most time for the clients—education about the legal system, realizing who they are and how they fit into the system, and developing realistic goals and some sense of having processed some of the emotional pain so that they can deal with the difficult decisions about their goals. It's a matter of dealing with pain; there is nobody that has an easy time with a divorce.

Lawyer Mary H. Wechsler, Wechsler Becker, LLP, Seattle, Washington

---

The most expensive parts of divorce are just getting people to get things done, whether it is your client or the other side, and irrational behavior. If I give clients tasks to do, and they don't get the tasks done, this increases costs. For example, not returning phone calls, being late to return a draft that required review, and just not following up on something. If I'm still waiting for you to give me something so I can complete a step that should have been taken care of long ago, some of the actions we could have taken subsequently will probably have passed us by, sometimes to the client's detriment. If a client acts out, that could also hurt the case and escalate costs.

Lawyer Stacy D. Phillips, Phillips, Lerner, Lauzon
& Jamra, Los Angeles, California

Keep a "Divorce Journal"

If you're in the midst of a divorce, or even contemplating one, consider keeping a journal of events for your lawyer. Note all events that you feel are relevant to your divorce and that may affect the outcome. These could be events that involve you or your children. You and your lawyer will want to refer to this journal to help you confirm relevant dates and information. You might want to include this information in affidavits, letters, and other written documents. This will help to show the accuracy of information and to validate dates, times, and other facts.

The journal might prove especially important if you end up going to trial. Judges don't know what really happened; they only know what the lawyers, through their clients, tell them. A diary of everything that happens during (and before) your divorce could be used as evidence if you go to court. The party that fails to keep such a journal is at a significant disadvantage.

Create a Meetings Notebook

What I found helpful in keeping me organized, refreshing my memory, and ensuring that I followed up on meetings and tasks was to create a notebook for my divorce. This book was divided into four sections:

1. meeting agendas and questions
2. notes from the meetings
3. next steps, or "to do" lists, with deadline dates, completion dates, and the date that each completed task or document was communicated or sent to my legal counsel
4. contacts, their phone numbers, and miscellaneous information

When creating and maintaining your own notebook, be sure to date everything.

I encourage people to bring somebody to all their meetings. Bring a friend, bring a relative. Typically the client sits there alone during the meeting, and when he or she gets home, Mom or a friend will ask, "What did the lawyer say?" All too often, the client's response is, "I don't know." The entire meeting went in one ear and out the other. Bring another person along who makes sure the business gets done, who hears what has to be heard. Very often people don't hear what is said to them. I may have said, "You're going to lose this motion." They walk out thinking everything's great. If they had somebody there with them, somebody who walks in understanding their concerns, that person will say, "That's not what he said." The client can still ignore it, but at least you've got a better chance of getting through. And sometimes someone who accompanies the client will give a slightly different account of the facts than the client does. It's a good tool for the lawyer. It's a good resource for the client. When carefully chosen, a good "significant other" can be very valuable.

Lawyer Lorne Wolfson, Torkin Manes, Toronto, Ontario

Set Up a Divorce Filing System

One of my personality quirks is that I like to be in control and know that important documents are easily accessible. This strategy certainly served me well when I was going through my divorce. Keep a file just like your lawyer does, with all the paperwork arranged in an orderly way. Your lawyer will ask you to refer to these papers many times, and your work will be easier and less stressful if you are organized and can easily reference what your lawyer is talking to you about.

Your filing system need not be anything complicated or expensive, and simple file folders are perfect. I happen to prefer legal-size folders, but use whatever works best for you. One way to start is to file all of your divorce-related paperwork, in chronological order, in folders that have specific headings that are relevant to your case. Here are some ideas for the headings you may want to set up:

- correspondence with lawyer, organized by date and topic
- orders or agreements

- folder for each member of your divorce team (financial expert, parenting expert, and so forth).
- financial statements—the statements of assets and liabilities
- invoices/statements—all costs associated with your divorce
- parenting plan
- discovery or deposition transcripts

If you want to get more detailed, you could arrange files more specifically—according to particular financial or child-related issues, for instance—but that depends on the issues that are being dealt with by your legal counsel or other professional team member. Of course, the detail you go into also depends on the type of divorce you're pursuing. For instance, you might not need a discovery or deposition file if you are not litigating.

Do Your Homework and Take Responsibility

No one knows your history better than you. It is up to you to inform your lawyer of all details. Don't be afraid to correct him or her if you think a piece of information was communicated incorrectly. Your lawyer will help you file specific documents and might phrase things in ways that are not factually correct. It is your job to read through the materials and ensure that everything in those documents is correct. If there are any errors, and the other side finds them, it could be a costly mistake.

Be honest with your lawyer. Don't withhold information from your lawyer because you heard from some other source that certain information might create problems for you. Don't avoid dealing with issues that you think are serious. The worst thing you can do in any matrimonial dispute is to withhold information. People use the fact that they are getting divorced or that they are emotionally upset or that they have a professional that's helping them—they use that sometimes as a way to avoid accountability. You have to be meticulous in the truthfulness of the information you present before the court. I think that people who misrepresent facts are setting themselves up for enormous problems. If you don't have credibility, that's the end of you. Lots of people have very bad situations. They've made enormous mistakes before they've come to see their lawyers, or even after they come to see their lawyers. The best possible thing they can do is to be honest with their lawyers and to work together with their lawyers to figure out, strategically, how they're going to deal with this.

Lawyer Brenda Christen, Wilson Christen, LLP, Toronto, Ontario

---

Remember, too, that your lawyer will advise and recommend, but will leave the final decision on any course of action to you, the client. According to many lawyers, clients do not want to take responsibility for the choices they've made. If your lawyer thinks you are making a bad decision, he or she will send you what lawyer Stacy D. Phillips, of Phillips, Lerner, Lauzon & Jamra in Los Angeles, California, calls a "CYA [cover your, ahem, derriere] letter," which ensures that the lawyer is off the hook for your poor decision. The letter is also designed to make you step back and reflect one more time in the hope that you might make a different decision. But the choice is still yours to make. Some clients can't accept this, and they will fire their lawyer and look for someone else who will make decisions for them.

If I think a client is about to make a poor decision, I will say, "This is not an argument; it is an exchange of information. I believe that you are about to make a serious error in judgment here. Let's get another opinion." But the final decision is the client's to make. Clients have a right to make a wrong decision.

Lawyer Mike McCurley, McCurley Orsinger
McCurley Nelson & Downing, LLP, Dallas, Texas

This is your case. I make recommendations and give advice; you make the final decisions. You do not have to take my advice; you only have to listen to it. I hope you will follow my advice, but you certainly are not required to do so. If I think you will place yourself in serious trouble by not following my advice, I will tell you. I may put it in writing and ask you to acknowledge receiving it. But, when we are done, you are going to be better informed and well equipped to make good decisions. You are going to understand the social science regarding child-related issues. You are also going to understand the impact of various personality profiles regarding the players in the divorce. Finally, you are going to understand the basics of valuation—what it means to have fifty-fifty property division or seventy-thirty property division—and some basic principles of taxation. We are going to do a lot of hands-on work (much on the computer), and please do not be bashful about asking questions. If I think the answer is too technical, and you do not really need to know it, I will tell you. If you want me to do more or explain more, I will certainly do it. I am just reminding you again that I charge on an hourly basis, so whenever you take my time you need to think about how cost-effective a particular exercise is likely to be. If you're not sure how to figure that out, ask the lawyer. Of course, he or she will always tell you. This candid communication is the essence of a good lawyer-client relationship.

Lawyer Allan R. Koritzinsky, Foley & Lardner, LLP, Madison, Wisconsin

How to Keep Your Legal Costs Down

The monthly statement from my lawyer's office was always the last piece of mail to get opened. Sometimes it would take me a few days to open it, and my fingers trembled when I finally did. Were there enough funds in the retainer to cover this bill? Did I need to submit additional money? Why couldn't I keep the bills down? Why did they add up to so much so quickly? Why? Why? Why? My frustration only grew.

It took me a while to figure out some cost-effective strategies. One day, during one of my many phone calls to my lawyer, he said to me, "Did you know that you are the client I receive the most calls from?" I was actually proud of myself. I thought it meant I was one of the clients most involved in his or her divorce; I thought it showed I really cared about what was happening. That is, until I received my statement. You see, the lawyer charges for every one of your calls, no matter how short or how inconsequential the question. One ten-minute call is cheaper than ten one-minute calls. So treat your calls to your lawyer like long-distance calls. Don't waste time on the little stuff, and get to the core of the matter immediately.

In addition, don't be afraid to ask questions if you don't agree with your monthly statement. I remember that the postage fee seemed quite high on one statement. Oops—turned out they'd accidentally added an extra "0." It was an honest but potentially costly mistake that was easily corrected. (If discussion fails to resolve your billing disagreement, the law may allow you to take your dispute to a public official for resolution. However, since doing so will likely mean the end of the business relationship between you and your lawyer, this method should probably be used only as a last resort.)

Here are some other strategies that I learned the hard way for keeping your bills down.

Maximize Your Meeting Time

- Schedule your meetings through your lawyer's assistant.
- Make a list of questions you would like to discuss, organized by topic or issue.

- Have an agenda ready, with all items and issues to be discussed.
- Take notes.
- Do any follow-up work the lawyer gives you (reviewing documents, contacting a specific specialist, and so forth), and make sure it is done in a timely manner.

Use your time efficiently. I often say to clients, "I've been with you for ten minutes now. You paid to come and meet with me. I still don't know why you're in my office. What is it that you have to ask me?" Then I have other clients that come and meet with me, and they never stop talking. I say the same thing: "You paid to come and meet with me, but you haven't given me a chance to say anything. I've heard your story, but what is it that you want from me?"

Lawyer Nancy Zalusky Berg, Walling
Berg & Debele, PA, Minneapolis, Minnesota

Make All Communications Cost-Effective

- Save up your questions. Don't call or e-mail your lawyer every single time you have an inquiry.
- Check with your lawyer first and find out how he or she likes to handle communications—via e-mail, phone calls, or meetings with prepared agendas. Also ask for recommendations on making your communications more efficient.

It's important to know when and how often to communicate. Some lawyers will say that there are people whom they never hear from, whom they would like to talk to more often, and other people they hear from five or ten times a day. Overcommunication will just escalate your legal bills and could hurt your relationship with your lawyer.

The client should organize his or her thoughts and questions and then talk to the lawyer. The client should work cooperatively and diligently with the lawyer to provide information. Avoid repeated telephone calls, but put together questions and present them at one time. Most importantly, the client should not take unreasonable positions or obdurately "stand on principle." It will escalate costs faster than almost anything else.

Lawyer Armin Kuder, Kuder, Smoller & Friedman, Washington D.C.

Provide as Much Written Information as Possible

Many lawyers have their clients write out an account of their marital history. That's because it is expensive for you to tell it to your lawyer personally in a meeting, and there may be things you will be able to remember and put into context better when writing. Some lawyers will assign clients other written tasks as well.

If I have a client who can do first drafts of documents themselves, that's fine. That's not just a function of education; it's also a function of how realistic people are and how well they can express themselves. But whatever work on their own cases clients can handle, I give to them.

Lawyer Mary H. Wechsler, Wechsler Becker, LLP, Seattle, Washington

---

Use Your Lawyer's Services Cost-Efficiently

- Listen to your lawyer and take notes.
- Remember, if you want to vent and complain about your soon-to-be ex-spouse, the meter is still running.

- If you are able to, do certain tasks, such as filling out the financial statement, yourself.
- Don't micromanage (pay extreme attention to the small details of) your case. This only causes your legal bills to escalate and slows down the process.

Some clients determine that they know more than the lawyer, and they've got to double-, triple- and quadruple-check everything that you do. And then they've got to change everything, and they are not happy. They don't understand the process; they want documents to contain their whole life story rather than the basic outline necessary for filing in court. They want to put all the evidence in, but it should be saved for court, and that's a big problem.

Lawyer Jack A. Rounick, Flamm, Boroff & Bacine, PC, Blue Bell, Pennsylvania

---

Do not insist that your lawyer do a specific job if he or she recommends that a junior lawyer, assistant, or other professional do it instead. I remember that for one of my many court dates, when we only had to appear to schedule another court date, my high-priced lawyer recommended that one of his juniors go in his place. I wanted my lawyer to be there, but he felt his appearance wasn't necessary. I followed his advice, and was glad I did, because it saved me a few hundred dollars.

Senior lawyers almost never do 100 percent of the work for clients. They may make most court appearances, and they may go to all the case conferences and settlement conferences, but they won't necessarily draft papers or do anything else that a junior or assistant can do, because it is economically impractical. Paralegals—individuals with specialized legal training who assist lawyers—are very efficient and are as well trained as the lawyers to handle the various filings, fees, and processes necessary to keep the divorce proceeding. You need to check the facts and details of every situation carefully, but the use of paralegals, assistants, and junior counsel is often a great way for you and your lawyer to control costs.

Try to be effective in the use of your time and the lawyers' time. Let your lawyer use the juniors or the law clerks when appropriate. Don't insist on the senior lawyers' time; it's foolish. Some clients won't let me delegate, and I say that's ridiculous. They want me to do something and I don't need to do it; it's a waste of money.

Lawyer Stephen Grant, McCarthy Tétrault, Toronto, Ontario

If you are developing a detailed parenting plan or addressing other parenting issues, most lawyers do not want to be involved with the specifics. How does your lawyer know if a Wednesday-night sleepover is best, or the best hours and location for transition times? Lawyers are not parenting experts. Besides, lawyers are far more expensive than most of the experts they recommend.

Pick the Battles That Make Sense

The cost-benefit approach to divorce battles is very helpful; if you want to do X, your lawyer can tell you that it will cost you Y dollars. Evaluate that information carefully and decide if it's worth it to proceed. This analysis can sometimes be a struggle when you enter the "gray zone"—when you're dealing with issues that are outside the parameters of the law or with costs that are not straightforward (for instance, if you're considering a child-related issue that has no concrete financial dimension). But weighing the decision practically rather than being led by your emotions will prevent the legal bills from escalating.

It helps to make sure you are not spending five thousand dollars to fight a seven-thousand-dollar issue, especially if you might not win.

Lawyer Mark S. Patt, Trope and Trope, Los Angeles, California

And don't keep changing your mind on positions you've already agreed on; it will only cost you more money.

What increases costs is clients who constantly change their minds. It is OK to change your mind based on new information. But a client who changes his or her mind after we have already vetted the decision and who marches off into ten different directions because he or she is unsure of that decision will cause problems and affect credibility with the other side and the court.

Lawyer Stacy D. Phillips, Phillips, Lerner,
Lauzon & Jamra, Los Angeles, California

Dealing with the "Phantom Board of Directors"

Sometimes people have not only their own emotions to contend with, but also the emotions of their friends and family, who may be trying to look out for them but who offer much unwanted and incorrect advice. Most everyone around you will have an opinion about the outcome of your settlement, and you may be pushed to do something different from what your lawyer is advising you to do.

Friends and family have likely heard and read about the outcomes of other people's divorces, and they often expect the process to work the same for you. But every case has its own set of particulars that your "advisory board" is not aware of. In addition, these people are generally not informed about the law. Another difficulty might be that your family and friends have their own agendas. They could be angry or fearful for you and offer you advice that is intended to be helpful, but is actually quite destructive.

Your family and friends only want what is in your best interests. The problem is that, realistically, they can't know what your best interests are from a legal standpoint. You need to bring all of their advice to your lawyer's office so he or she can help you sort it out. That will produce an outcome that works.

A lot of clients have what I call a "phantom board of directors." Perhaps their neighbor had a case, and the neighbor says, "That's ridiculous, I never paid that amount of child support; you shouldn't be paying that amount of child support." Or the sister says, "You should do this," or, "Don't even bother" when you want to bother, so clients get all kinds of conflicting advice. I call them the "phantom board" because I don't know who these people are, but I know they're influencing my client. If there is somebody that is really important, I bring them into the process; perhaps it's the client's father who is paying the bill, or a trusted friend.

Lawyer Nicole Tellier, Nicole Tellier Law Offices, Toronto, Ontario

---

Working with Your Lawyer to Deal with a Problem Ex

Where your soon-to-be-former spouse is in the grieving cycle (discussed in chapter 2) has a tremendous impact on how he or she reacts during the divorce process. Maybe your ex is acting out of revenge, guilt, or fear. Maybe he or she exhibits mental instability, is narcissistic, or has borderline personality disorder or some other emotional dysfunction. If so, what do you do? Ideally, you've got an experienced lawyer who can recognize the potential issues and who knows how to deal with them.

I come across two types of narcissism. I call it the big N and the little n. The big N shows up, of course, when we run into people who have narcissistic personality disorder. The little-n type of narcissism shows up because divorce induces a certain amount of narcissism even in fairly normal people. In the last couple of years of a marriage, people are not treating each other with dignity and with a sense of sensitivity to them being real human beings. They're usually treating each other like negative objects by that time. We get a lot of really normal people who are in a really narcissistic phase as a result of the divorce process, and so they show the symptoms of narcissism—the sense of entitlement, the kind of unrealistic expectations of getting more attention than everybody else, and so on. But once the situation calms down, and we can get them focused on some future goals, and get them focused on working together as parents, usually that artificial narcissism begins to calm down.

Psychologist Dr. Ken Waldron, Waldron
Kriss and Associates, Madison, Wisconsin

When dealing with a problem ex, it's especially critical to choose your battles carefully. Work with your lawyer to determine what's most important, and don't respond to everything. Focus on the big picture. If custody is the most important issue, don't get stuck fighting about one hundred dollars in your property division.

I try to work with a client's therapist. Some people are true victims. What you have to look out for are perpetual victims, because they will continue to use their exes to victimize themselves. I have clients who have to deal with personality dysfunction from the other side. What I tell them is, "You have to realize that you are never going to change your ex-spouse, and you cannot control your ex's behavior." My clients might feel as though they are being made to appear crazy or are being gaslighted. You have to analyze each case, each client, each opposing side, and the people who are surrounding the opposing side.

Lawyer Stacy D. Phillips, Phillips, Lerner, Lauzon & Jamra,

Los Angeles, California

Do you remember the old romantic thriller *Gaslight*, starring Charles Boyer and Ingrid Bergman? It's about a woman who thinks she is losing her grip on reality, when in fact her husband is intentionally trying to drive her insane. The term "gaslight" is used to refer to any deliberate attempt to drive another person crazy. The concept of gaslighting offers an interesting way to look at what can happen in a high-conflict divorce scenario. All too often, certain tactics from your soon-to-be-former spouse or his or her counsel are constructed to throw you off balance, keep you on the defensive, and ultimately, get you to question your own reactions. Possible gaslighting tactics include slinging slanderous and false allegations and writing very intimidating, nasty letters to which your side is forced to respond.

Our whole culture is geared toward the idea that divorce means a fight. All of our culture is imbued with that. People should look at what they are doing when they are buying into that cultural norm of divorce, and what they are doing to themselves and their children.

Psychologist Dr. Peggy Thompson, Family

Psychological Services, Orinda, California

Ethically, I wonder how a lawyer could participate in such actions, which foster an adversarial relationship and which don't serve the best interests of the family. Some lawyers would consider this behavior self-serving.

Lawyers have their own biases, blind spots, and agendas all too often. I find cases that should be settled, that are simple, that are not that complex—they are being exacerbated and extended by lawyers who have all kinds of issues with regard to winning and competition. Very often it's not about what's best for the client; it's about boosting the reputation of the lawyer. To help a client who is not psychologically ready to handle the divorce process is a big mistake, and it happens all too often.

Lawyer Ronald Supancic, Family Law Offices of
Ronald M. Supancic, Woodland Hills, California

On the other hand, clients very often look for lawyers whose personality styles match their own. If your spouse is feeling angry and aggressive, he or she will most likely look for a lawyer who has a reputation for being angry and aggressive. On the other hand, a client who is looking to resolve things and negotiate amicably will probably look for a lawyer who he or she believes will do the same.

Your partner—your husband or your wife—will find a lawyer who is like him or her. If a husband has been horrible and head butting and abusive, he will hire a lawyer just like that. If a wife is picky and wants to fight over every little thing, she is going to find a lawyer just like that. That often happens.

Lawyer Carole Curtis, Carole Curtis Law Offices, Toronto, Ontario

Although this knowledge provides little relief or comfort at the time when you are experiencing torment—and spending money to defend yourself—I hope it will provide you with the strength to know that you are not alone and that you can get through it intact, especially when you surround yourself with your support team. Try not to get hooked into battle by reacting emotionally, but instead focus on providing information that could help defuse the situation. If you think you're going to have allegations made against you, keep a journal, keep good records, and be ready to respond when someone says you did something a week or two ago that you did not do.

My mantra is, "Don't take it personally." Whatever your spouse is doing, he or she is doing it for his or her own reasons and interests, and not because of you. That is the idea I try to get across. Therefore, the client should be creating goals for himself or herself, and implementing strategies to accomplish those goals insofar as they are reasonable and possible. Let the other side do what they think they must do, but don't take that personally.

Lawyer Armin Kuder, Kuder, Smoller & Friedman, Washington, D.C.

You might be feeling overwhelming distress, and it may seem that the conflict will never end. The idea of "fight or flight" might kick in—you are tired of fighting, so you want to run away from the situation. Take reassurance in knowing that no matter how bad things get, no matter how bad you feel, running away will only make things worse. In fact, if the other side is unable to negotiate, sometimes it is better to slow down the process. Many therapists would advise that, strategically, if you give the other side some time to process what is happening, you might actually negotiate a better settlement, be more amicable, and get through the whole ordeal sooner than you will if you pressure the other side to move as quickly as you would like to.

The process is neither self-generating, nor a snowball going down a hill. The way the process moves forward is, to some extent, directed by the parties collectively, and by the court's ability to move things along on its own. Frequently, one party wants the process to go forward faster than the other, but he or she usually understands that in order for the process to be most successful and produce the least amount of strain, he or she must respect—or at least recognize—the other party's need for reasonable timing. You might want the case to be done yesterday, but it's reasonable to give the other party enough time to gather and review all the information necessary to make informed decisions.

Lawyer Dianna Gould-Saltman, Gould-Saltman
Law Offices, LLP, Los Angeles, California

Be aware, though, that the other side may follow a similar strategy. There may be a time when you feel your ex is stalling the case, but it may in fact be his or her lawyer who is stalling the case, in an attempt to create the proper timing for that lawyer's plans. One thing good lawyers do is time things strategically.

Clients don't understand it. Every psychiatrist will explain to you that there are more strategic times to make deals and less strategic times to make deals. For instance, when one party feels guilty and the other party feels angry, if you represent the angry party, you want to close the deal as quickly as possible, because the guilty party will probably give you more than he or she would normally give you. If you represent the guilty party, you want to slow down the litigation; if you don't, your client will give up the ship to the angry party out of a sense of remorse and in order to avoid the ex's apparent anger.

Lawyer Steven A. Mindel, Feinberg, Mindel, Brandt,
Klein & Kline, LLP, Los Angeles, California

Sometimes an ex's difficult behavior is rooted not in strategy, but in an actual personality dysfunction. While true dysfunction is a factor in only a small percentage of cases, it is important to understand that such problems do occasionally play a role, and can cause resolution to become extremely difficult. They raise blaming, victimization, and revenge to a whole different level.

To my surprise, the issues I encountered in family court were the same mental health issues that I was working with as a therapist. And the more I examined how cases progressed, the more it seemed to me that the issues were not so much about the law, but more about mental health problems—especially when dealing with people with traits of personality disorders who had very rigid thinking and really had difficulty feeling loss and viewing situations in terms of compromise. I realized that other lawyers and judges, and even therapists, had no clue that these issues played a role. If a person's own lawyer really doesn't understand a problematic ex's issues, there are two approaches that person can take to handle the situation. One is to try to get a mental health professional who does understand involved in the case. Some mental health professionals, especially ones involved in the court system, are able to explain to the lawyers what's going on. The other approach is to find a lawyer who is more sensitive to those issues.

Mediator and lawyer William A. Eddy, National
Conflict Resolution Center, San Diego, California

The way to handle an ex's personality dysfunction is to learn about the dynamics of his or her personality disorders or traits so you can work with your lawyer to predict the kinds of crises you're likely to face. According to many therapists, many such crises really are predictable.

Divorce is a crazy-making time, and sometimes your own behavior might be erratic. Your lawyer can protect you by telling you if you are out of line. Clients that have unresolved emotional agendas, lawyers would say, are very difficult to work with, and so working with mental health professionals is really a crucial element to good outcomes.

Always remember, winning doesn't simply mean getting a reasonable settlement. It means something more than that—more than achieving a goal at a burdensome price. For example, a client may achieve far more if he can just exercise some restraint and curb a seemingly uncontrollable need to pound someone into the ground.

Lawyer Glenn C. Lewis, Lewis Law Firm, Washington, D.C.

Now that you've learned some things about choosing and working with your lawyer, parenting throughout divorce, and taking charge of your emotions, what's next in your quest to have a smart divorce? It's time to turn your attention to taking charge of your finances.

7

Taking Control
of Your Finances

The uncoupling of a husband and wife has a significant financial impact. What was once an income shared by two in one
household is now divided to support two households.

Taking control of and managing my household finances was
empowering. It felt great to make all of the financial decisions, pay
the bills, and know what was happening with the little budget that
I had. There was so much to do, but I knew where to start, because
I was organized, and organization is the key to being in control.

Understanding the Division of Assets

Each state or jurisdiction deals with division of family assets differently. Generally speaking, when separation occurs, the couple's
financial statements are used to help assess each party's financial worth, based on assets and liabilities accumulated during the
marriage. The next step is for the spouse with more assets (the
payor spouse) to pay the spouse with fewer assets (the *recipient
spouse*) so that they each end up with an equal share of the assets
from the period of their marriage. This is called the *equalization
payment*.

Spousal support, also referred to as alimony or maintenance support, is a separate financial consideration. It consists of ongoing payments from one spouse to the other on a short- or long-term basis. The payments are designed to meet the financial needs of the recipient spouse at the date of separation and to put each member of the divorcing couple in the same financial situation he or she was in prior to the separation. Entitlement to spousal support depends on each spouse's circumstances and is not a given. It is based on a *needs test*, which determines the amount of money that a potential recipient spouse requires in order to maintain the lifestyle he or she had at the date of separation, and the amount the payor spouse has the ability to pay.

Spousal support is usually paid to compensate a homemaker, whose career has been to stay home and take care of the children. It may also be paid to a spouse who developed a disability during the marriage and who now cannot be self-supporting. If one spouse has a paying job but the other spouse is significantly wealthier, the wealthier party may still have to pay some support so the ex can maintain the lifestyle the couple enjoyed during the marriage.

Spousal support usually continues as long as the payor spouse has the ability to pay or until the recipient spouse becomes self-sufficient. In most cases payment ceases upon the remarriage or death of the recipient spouse. Agreements are sometimes negotiated in which payments are made even after the party receiving the maintenance remarries, but this arrangement must be spelled out specifically in the divorce agreement. The same is true for continuing payments beyond the recipient spouse's death, but the recipient spouse must structure an estate plan to accommodate that.

If the payor spouse dies while payments are still being made, they will most likely continue, covered by the payor's life insurance or otherwise charged against his or her estate. However, if the estate does not have the funds, the recipient spouse could end up losing the support.

Spousal support is often awarded in cases in which one spouse has put his or her education or career on hold in order to raise the parties' children while the other climbed the career ladder and achieved a higher income. In such cases, the alimony will often be temporary, providing income for the period of time that will enable the recipient spouse to become self-supporting. This temporary, or rehabilitative, spousal support enables the spouse receiving it to further his or her education, reestablish himself of herself in a former career, or complete childrearing responsibilities, after which time he or she can be self-sufficient. If one spouse is unable to get a good-paying job, however, due perhaps to health or advanced age, the support award may be permanent.

Lawyer Nancy Zalusky Berg, Walling
Berg & Debele, PA, Minneapolis, Minnesota

Child support, on the other hand, is not about giving money to your spouse; it's about providing for your children. I don't understand why there is often a battle to collect the funds for child support. It just shouldn't happen. You made the commitment to have children; this responsibility includes financially supporting your children as well.

The amount of child support a payor is required to provide is usually clear-cut, as there are guidelines based on the payor's income. If, in future years, the payor's tax return reflects a significant change in income, either party can request an adjustment to the child support arrangement. If the payor becomes more financially successful postdivorce, the children are entitled to a share of the increased wealth of their parent. Look at it this way: If you were all living together, the children would be growing up in a nice house that featured all sorts of recreational properties and other bells and whistles. The rationale is that they should not be deprived of this now. Check with your lawyer to learn how to request child support adjustments once the separation agreement has been signed.

Organizing Your Finances

All lawyers agree on how important it is for their clients to be as financially aware as possible. It's the best way to learn your rights and obligations and to determine realistic expectations early in the divorce process. Once you have a handle on your financial situation, your lawyer can give you informed opinions based on fact, not on speculation. And the more you can manage and organize your information for your lawyer and establish realistic financial goals, the more you can help reduce your lawyer's billable hours.

Organizing your finances can be difficult if you were not the one responsible for them during your marriage—if you were what some lawyers call the *noninformed spouse*. If possible, try to become more financially aware before you separate:

- Get more involved in your finances. Know the basics—pay the bills and file the statements. Learn how your daily and monthly expenses are managed.
- Determine where the money is coming from and how it is applied toward your budget.
- Take part in setting up investments such as retirement funds, and understand where and what the other assets are.

Many lawyers suggest that if someone is contemplating a divorce or separating, one of the first things he or she should do is accumulate the financial information.

Gather Your Financial Documents

Once the divorce process is under way, your lawyer will need ready access to all relevant financial documents. Start by locating and gathering together the following records pertaining to both you and your spouse:

- social security numbers
- income tax returns for the past three years
- retirement savings plans statements for the past three years
- bank account statements
- insurance policies (life; automobile; house; other)
- stock certificates
- credit card bills
- employment payment stubs
- brokerage statements
- pension statements
- health insurance and work-related benefits
- real estate records
- receipts and monthly statements documenting household expenses and everyday expenses (groceries, gas, heat, water, personal grooming, transportation, gifts, clothing, laundry and cleaning supplies, entertainment, miscellaneous expenses, and so forth)
- list of all assets and liabilities
- date of separation (the date of separation, or "valuation date," is the date that is used to determine the value of particular assets—the matrimonial home, bank statements, investments, and so forth)

Photocopy everything, and store your set in a separate folder from the original records. Don't just keep the originals for your own personal use; the other side is entitled to these documents, too. If you do withhold these records from the other side, sooner or later you are going to be asked to provide them, which will cost you even more in legal fees.

The financially noninformed spouse is often the one who is left in the house in the first days or weeks after separation. That would be a good time to make copies of all of these records. Keep your set outside of your home—perhaps at a trusted friend's house or in your own personal safety deposit box. Return the original documents to the family files, but build the paper trail while you have access to the documents.

What if your former partner has made off with the financial records? Before you start sending letters back and forth, try doing what you can to find them or to reassemble the information yourself. Look in a shared safety deposit box or in the family filing cabinet. Ask your banker, broker, or financial adviser to provide the missing data. Retrieve household statements from the companies that provide the services, such as the phone company. The more financial information you can pass along to your lawyer, the better.

Set Up a Financial Filing System

When my lawyer's office asked me to fill out a financial statement, they were extremely surprised at how quickly, accurately, and efficiently I was able to do so. My secret was an extremely simple filing system that I've now been using for twenty-five years: an expandable file folder with thirty-one tabs on it. Each tab corresponds to a different item or company that is relevant to my personal finances. I start a new one every year, and store the old ones away.

To start a filing system of your own, label the front of your file folder with a key for easy reference. Here's an example of a system you might use:

Year _____

1. income tax receipts
2. property tax assessments
3. mortgage statements
4. home insurance statements

5. life insurance policies
6. bank account statements (savings and checking)
7. retirement fund statements
8. other investments (you could have one tab per investment)
9. credit card statements (you could have one tab per credit card)
10. loans or lines of credit
11. medical expenses
12. children's bank or investment accounts
13. children's school information and expenses
14. children's summer program information and expenses
15. children's other program information and expenses
16. children's extraordinary expenses
17. car costs (insurance statements, maintenance receipts, etc.)
18. phone bills (home and cell)
19. cable/satellite, Internet, and other computer-related information and expenses
20. home alarm system information and statements
21. gas, water, and other utility statements (you could have one tab per utility)
22. other home expenses
23. charitable donations
24. miscellaneous receipts
25. other

If you can pull all of this information together and organize it yourself, you'll gain credibility when you fill out your financial statement, because you'll have documentation to support the information you submit. You'll also have an easy way to forecast next year's expenses. In addition, you will be able to fill out your financial statement on your own, without the assistance of legal staff, which will again save you time and money.

You may have specific documents that you'll want to refer to five years from now, and if you put them in your annual folder they may be forgotten. In this case, you may want to create another file folder for any documents that you don't file away at the end of the year.

Here's an example of the system you might use for this folder:

1. divorce decree
2. final separation agreement
3. final parenting plan
4. last will and testament
5. bank accounts
6. property deeds
7. other

You can also use computer programs such as Quicken to help you organize your financial information.

Establish Your Own Financial Identity

If you have been the financially noninformed spouse, and you do not have a credit rating, now is the time to start building one. (Note that credit cards only affect the credit rating of each card's principal holder; you may find yourself with no credit rating even if you and your spouse had joint credit card accounts.) If you are in the matrimonial home and your spouse has left, you might want to consider putting the household bills in your name. Make sure you pay these off on time and in full. This is a good way to start establishing a good credit rating. Apply for your own credit card. If you are a first-time card holder, you can always start out with a small credit limit and gradually increase it as you regularly pay your bill on time and prove to be a good credit risk.

Make friends with your banker and borrow five hundred dollars. That's usually possible without any collateral. Make sure you pay back the loan in accordance with the terms of the agreement. Once it's paid off, take out another loan—this time for eight hundred or a thousand dollars (again, with no collateral)— and make sure it is paid off quickly. What you're doing is building credit with your bank. You're building credit every place. Make sure that all bills are paid on time.

Certified Financial Planner Carol Ann Wilson,
Carol Ann Wilson, LLC, Boulder, Colorado

The next step should be to set up your own bank account, especially if you currently have only a joint account with your spouse. Before you tap into any family money, consult with your own lawyer to make sure he or she approves.

Assuming there are no prior restraining orders in effect, if there is cash available, either half the amount should be moved to a new account that is controlled by the client, or sufficient funds should be withdrawn from the existing account to provide security for that client for the immediate future.

Lawyer Stephen A. Kolodny, Kolodny & Anteau, Beverly Hills, California

---

As for your life insurance or other insurance coverage, keep in mind that if you cancel an existing policy, you may not be able to secure coverage later on because it will be too expensive or disallowed due to age or poor health. You should also check with your lawyer before changing beneficiaries on specific policies.

Creating a Realistic Monthly Budget

You may have already prepared a monthly budget for your lawyer to review. If not, you soon will. Having a budget is also a smart way to help you maintain control of your finances as you move forward.

The financial files you created—and the financial awareness they helped to foster—will help with your budget preparations. But you also need to be forward thinking and consider expenses that you may not have had to pay previously but may need to pay now, such as health insurance, car insurance, home insurance, or life insurance policies. Some of these costs may have been covered by a spouse's business when you were married but now need to be included in your monthly budget.

Most people want to maintain the lifestyle they had while married, but oftentimes they are not aware of how this lifestyle was funded. Maybe it was financed through unsound means. If your lifestyle was paid for with generous family gifts or incurred debt, such as credit card debt, bank loans, or a second mortgage, it may be unrealistic to maintain that standard of living postdivorce. And if you are the one to receive spousal or child support, you need to make that money last. You may have to scale back your budget dramatically. Really think it through to determine what you need to do to work within your means. Also, don't forget to set aside money to pay your income tax if you haven't been responsible for that in the past.

If you don't know how to set up and manage your finances, ask a trusted adviser or friend to help set you up. Or call on an accountant or financial planner—more information on working with these experts appears below.

Advice from Financial Experts

The financial issues associated with divorce can be complex. Without the proper guidance, you could find yourself in an adverse situation later on, when it is too late to do something about it. That is why your lawyer may recommend that you work with different financial experts to help you through this difficult time.

If your spouse agrees to full financial disclosure, then in most instances all you need to do is hire the appropriate expert to critique the numbers. If, on the other hand, you need to uncover financial information that is being withheld, remember that the more you ask your experts to do, the more it is actually going to cost you. Think about how much you are willing to spend and how much you may be able to uncover. Do the cost-benefit analysis, and don't fall prey to the "revenge factor." For example, are you going to spend ten thousand dollars to uncover five thousand, or will you spend thirty thousand dollars to find five hundred thousand?

Different experts have different training and expertise. Here are some things to know about each.

Accountants

An accountant is skilled at managing business records and sometimes at providing financial advice. He or she may prepare a client's tax returns. You or your spouse may have an accountant who you feel is qualified to provide you with all of the financial information that your lawyer requests.

However, many lawyers believe that if you rely on your own accountant to provide this information, you're making a mistake that will end up costing you more money in the long run. Your accountant can provide you with the basic financial facts, but he or she may not necessarily be familiar with family law rules or have the expertise to uncover all the information you're looking for. Furthermore, if you end up in court, the judge may not consider your personal accountant a "good" witness.

If you and your spouse use the same accountant, even the *information* that accountant provides may not be seen by your lawyer or the judge as totally independent and unbiased. In addition, conflict of interest may prevent him or her from testifying on your behalf.

Forensic Accountants

A forensic accountant, or litigation accountant, has additional training that allows him or her to investigate and analyze accounting information and prepare reports that can be used in court. There are different levels of investigation that can be pursued, with each level costing more money. These experts can help you to value things such as the interest in private companies, options, company public stock, and business assets.

Because of their expertise, forensic accountants are considered excellent witnesses in court. In addition, the information they provide can also help the parties come to a negotiated settlement and determine how the settlement amount is going to be paid. They evaluate the family assets and determine which ones are best to liquidate, transfer, or otherwise manipulate to meet the parties' financial obligations.

Financial Planners

The financial planner can analyze settlement options, explain how those options will affect your financial standing in the long term, and help you to manage your postdivorce financial plan to achieve your goals. The financial planner can help you develop accurate predivorce and postdivorce budgets to make sure that the numbers you report make sense. They can also help you understand your investments and how they should be managed.

Other Finance Experts

To accurately estimate your assets and liabilities, you may also need the help of other experts with training in specific areas. To value a pension, you would use a pension valuator. To value income from property investments, you would use a real estate appraiser. Whatever the item in question is, it is important to go to the professional who can best assess its value.

There are also experts who can help with your finances once the divorce is finalized. For instance, a money manager can maintain your investment portfolio by choosing which assets to buy or sell over time.

Finances of the Settlement

There is no crystal ball that will forecast exactly what the final outcome of the divorce process will be. Until the financial settlement is signed, you don't know what it is going to look like. When people assume that their settlement is going to result in X dollars and make investments or buy a home in anticipation of that outcome, they often regret their decisions when the settlement turns out to be smaller. In addition, monies you spend now might not be considered part of the marital assets—you might be held personally responsible for the expenses. Don't make any investments or major purchases prior to signing the final agreement.

There is a lot to think about before you sign: What are the tax implications of dividing property? Are the assumptions you used to calculate investment returns realistic? What legal fees or other expenses do you need to budget for? Take the time to consider all the options.

The family home is an especially difficult consideration. In most instances, your home represents more than just a roof over your head. For many, there are emotional ties, fond memories, and feelings of security. And the world around you assumes that in a divorce, the winner takes the home and the loser moves out. But, while the home represents so much emotionally, it may not be the best asset for your financial security. There are factors that need to be evaluated. What is the outstanding mortgage? Will your postdivorce income cover the costs to run your home? If you need to sell the home, what are the associated selling costs? Consider these factors, and discuss them with your experts when developing your postdivorce financial plan.

If you go to trial and a judge orders the equalization payment, in most cases that payment will need to be made in cash. If you are the payor spouse, you will be ordered to pay whatever the judge determines, so you need to have the cash on hand, or you will most likely have to liquidate some assets. In most instances, the payor is responsible for the taxes on this payment to the recipient.

Once all the financial agreements have been signed, you'll need to manage your postdivorce settlement to ensure that it lasts as long as you need it. You might want to consider contacting a money manager to help you sort out what to do next with your funds to help maintain your financial security.

8

Custody and Co-parenting Arrangements and Issues

Perhaps I'm sensitive, but I don't consider my children to be growing up in a "broken home" or any of the other terms the professionals call it. When I talk to my children, we refer to ourselves as a family, because that is what we are. We do not evaluate ourselves against the traditional family—the family with two parents living at home. Divorce may change a family's structure, but it is still a family, and all families have their challenges, no matter how they are configured. Your challenge is to make life just as normal as possible and to ensure that your children don't see themselves as "children of divorce" but just as regular children.

People need to think about their roles in their family of origin. What did you do? Who were you? What responsibilities did you have? What traditions did you have? Which of those do you want to keep, and which of those would you like to change? What new traditions would you like to create that would redefine you and the children as a family unit, without sending the message that what goes on in the other parent's household is "all wrong"? There are some differences between households. There are a number of categories that prompt parents to think, "How do I want this family to be defined, both in the context of the kids and their relationship with me and in the context of my co-parental relationship with the other person?" I think you need to be careful about wording here, because to these children, "family" still includes both parents. It's just that the parents are not in the same relationship. They are now in a co-parenting relationship.

Psychologist Dr. Karen Irvin, St. Paul, Minnesota

Understanding the Terminology

Parents have both rights and responsibilities concerning their children. They must make decisions regarding their children's health, education, and religion; support their children financially; and provide their children with a home. During the divorce process, however, the terms used to describe these rights and responsibilities can get confusing. Concepts often get mixed up, and definitions vary. As a result, parental expectations can become unclear. For example, recipient parents often assume that if the former spouse fails to pay child support, he or she will lose the right to see the children. But child support payment and visitation rights are two unrelated concepts; if payment is not made, the payor still has his or her visitation rights. It can be difficult emotionally for the recipient parent when the payor parent does not take his or her child support payments seriously but retains all of the other rights of parenting, but that's the way it is.

In addition, the legal terms used by the lawyers, judges, and other professionals can sound so cold and clinical that they are difficult to hear. The experts may refer to you not as "parents" but as your children's "decision makers." Instead of discussing the time you have to spend with the kids, they may talk about "access." I have never ever heard parents refer to their parental authority or to time with their kids in such detached ways. Nonetheless, it is important to understand these terms.

Custody

Custody refers to who has the legal authority to make decisions regarding a child's health, education, religion, and so forth. Generally speaking, custody does not establish residential status or access (visitation rights); those specifics are usually determined by the parenting plan (see page 138). However, the children's residential arrangements may differ depending on who has custody, and in cases in which the safety of the child is in question, a court's custody ruling may order that one parent have only supervised visitation, or no visitation at all.

Joint custody means that both parents retain legal decision-making authority. If parents with joint custody have a problem coming to a decision about the child's best interests, this can be resolved by a parenting expert such as an arbitrator or parenting coordinator.

Sole or *full custody* means that only one parent is given decision-making authority over the children, usually because it would be too difficult for the parents to make these decisions together. Needless to say, if you have sole custody, you must be especially careful to act in the best interests of your children. Usually, but not always, the decision-making parent is obligated to keep the other parent informed about the decisions made regarding the children.

Grandparent Access

In part because many of today's grandparents are young, fit, and healthy, and because most have some money and time that they would like to spend on their grandchildren, grandparent access is becoming a significant issue in society. When a marriage breaks down and the grandparents have problems coordinating with their own child to arrange visits with their grandchildren, they some-times go to court to gain access.

There is resistance to the notion that grandparents have rights regarding their grandchildren that are separate from the rights of the children's parents. Lawyers generally agree that grandparents should make arrangements to see the kids when their own child, the parent, has access to the grandchildren. However, even if their relationship with their own child is so dysfunctional that they can't do so, the court shouldn't get involved. Grandparents are fabulous for children; their role should not be diminished. However, there is only so much time in the children's post-separation lives as they move back and forth between their parents' homes, and to overlay that with another appointment, even if it's one with the grandparents, is a lot for the children to cope with.

The Children's Lawyer

The Office of the Children's Lawyer or the Office of the Guardian ad Litem is a government service offering justice on behalf of children under the age of eighteen with respect to their personal and property rights. The office provides a lawyer who represents the child in court, so he or she has a voice independent of the parents' legal interests. The lawyer's mandate is to do whatever is in the child's best interests.

If you are considering the involvement of this office, you need to think it through carefully and discuss the possibility with your lawyer. While a children's lawyer is needed in some cases, in others it just adds another layer of interference. Some lawyers feel the use of a children's lawyer can be a double-edged sword. If the children's lawyer gets involved in the process and supports you, you're golden. If he or she gets involved and sides against you, it can make things very difficult.

The truth is, during the conflict there is little way for children to have a voice in the process.

What parents should do is create freedom for their children by disengaging, and try to teach their children to be emancipated.

Lawyer Jeffery Wilson, Wilson Christen, LLP, Toronto, Ontario.

The Parenting Plan

The parenting plan is an agreement between divorcing parents that clearly defines how each is to continue caring for his or her children following a separation. The goals of the parenting plan are to encourage the children's relationship with both parents and to protect the children from parental conflict. It can also be used as an intervention tool to help parents disengage from one another. Parents often fear losing control or being controlled, and a specific, structured plan can help quell those feelings.

The parenting plan provides a comprehensive schedule of each parent's access to the children, outlines his or her co-parenting responsibilities, and establishes his or her role in parental decision making. The particulars of the plan depend on the relationship between the former spouses, each parent's relationship with his or her children, and, of course, the children's needs. It can be very detailed, and it may address questions such as the following:

- How should the parents communicate with each other? Verbally or in writing? Via e-mail?
- What religious tradition will the children follow?
- How do the children transition from one parent's home to the other? Where and when does a parent pick up and drop off the children?
- Who pays for gifts and celebrations (e.g., birthday parties)?
- How do the parents decide whether to sign the children up for extracurricular programs?
- What happens if parents don't agree on specific issues?

The parenting plan can configure the residential arrangement in a variety of ways. In some families, children split their time fifty-fifty between their mother's home and their father's. In other cases, the children live most of the time at one parent's home, which is called the *primary residence*; that parent is called the *primary residential parent*. The other parent, called the *secondary residential parent*, may have the children on select weekends and perhaps one day a week, and maybe on alternating holidays. There are, of course, many different ways to configure parental responsibility, and there is no right or wrong method.

A parenting plan can be developed in a number of ways. If the two parents get along and are on the same page on most issues, they may develop the plan together. This is a great situation to be in, because parents know their children best and will not have to rely on a third party to tell them how to parent. That doesn't mean they can't have some help developing the plan; there are many excellent experts who can help parents look at issues they might not have considered, work out creative solutions to problems, and keep an eye on future needs so that problems are avoided later on. But if parents prefer to work through a plan themselves, there are many books and Web sites to help them research the subject (see "Resources," pages 188, 191.

In such cases, the parents—not the children—should decide which home is the primary residence. You do not want to burden your children by forcing them to choose one parent over the other. That puts an incredible amount of pressure on them, which they will resent later on. Of course, children do sometimes take it upon themselves to voice their preferences. Especially if the child is an older teenager, his or her desires should be carefully considered when determining that child's best interests.

If the divorcing spouses do not agree on parenting responsibilities or residence issues, or if there are allegations of abuse, the parenting plan may be determined by a neutral third party—an evaluator who conducts a *custody and access assessment*.

Custody and Access Assessments

A custody and access assessment can be ordered by a judge or recommended by the parties' lawyers as a settlement tool. In this process, a custody evaluator interviews and observes all those involved in the parenting process and creates a detailed parenting plan. He or she may also recommend therapy, share ideas on developing parenting skills, and point out issues that need to be worked on.

The evaluation process is divided into six parts. In the first stage, the evaluator interviews the couple together, discussing their marriage and their values, what drew the couple together in the first place, and what broke them apart. This is followed by individual interviews with each parent. Then, at the evaluator's office (sometimes behind a two-way mirror), the evaluator watches each parent play, on separate occasions, with his or her children. The evaluator then visits each of the parent's homes. In the next stage, the evaluator reviews any documentation provided. Finally, he or she interviews "collaterals." Collaterals may be siblings, parents, teachers, babysitters, close friends—anyone who is familiar with the parents and who can provide some insight into the family dynamics or the parties' parenting abilities.

A custody and access assessment provides an opportunity for a neutral, unbiased, trained third party to accumulate a lot of information about everyone, sort through any allegations, and come to as clear an understanding as possible of how this family is functioning. It answers questions and concerns about what is going on with the children and why, which allows the evaluator to make a whole host of recommendations and present all of that information to the lawyers, and then to their clients, so that they can make use of it in trying to settle the case. A well-done custody evaluation is a significant piece of evidence.

Psychologist Dr. Benjamin M. Schutz, Springfield, Virginia

Having been through a custody and access evaluation, I understand its necessity. But that doesn't change the fact that I felt like I was in a fishbowl. I felt as though my judgment, lifestyle, parenting skills, decisions both past and present, and relationships with my children and everyone else were being dissected under a microscope. The evaluator judged me on how I played with my children and how they responded to me, and gauged the comfort level of my children in their own home. And the result was a parenting plan over which neither I nor my former spouse had any direct input. The outcome for me was positive, but did the end justify the means? While it was an uncomfortable situation to be in, I guess there was no choice. It prevented us from having to go to court and litigate custody; it was the option of last resort.

I don't want to scare you; only a small percentage of the divorcing population goes through a custody and access evaluation. This is not for the typical divorce. But for those who do have to go through it, it can be a difficult and invasive experience, and many people enlist the help of their own therapists to deal with the emotions. If you don't have a therapist, talking it through with a trusted adviser or friend could be very helpful.

What Makes a Good Custody Evaluator?

Most lawyers have a small pool of experts from which to recommend a custody evaluator, but who you choose can be extremely important to the family. You want someone with a lot of experience, someone who is honest, thorough, competent, and highly regarded by the legal community. This person must really understand the research collected and be focused on the children's best interests.

The evaluator will try to understand the parent's values while not imposing his or her own. Their role is to evaluate and report, not to provide therapy. While there are guidelines as to how the custody and access evaluation is conducted, custody evaluators have their own styles, philosophies, and procedures for getting it done. Some evaluators look at the situation solely from the perspective of uncovering the truth behind any allegations. Other evaluators take a broader look at the family dynamics and the environment that the children live in.

What to Tell the Children About the Assessment Process

You might tell your children that you are taking them to talk to someone about what is going on in your family; this person is going to make some recommendations and give you some ideas to help your family live in two separate homes. Assure your children that there is nothing to be afraid of; that this person will just ask them some questions that they should feel free to answer honestly.

Whether it's a judge, a lawyer, or a parent making the decisions, the focus is on finding some magic parenting plan—the perfect plan. The truth is that there is no one right plan. The focus needs to be on parenting and co-parenting. The answer isn't found in parenting arrangements; the answer is found in parenting relationships that make sense.

Professor of Psychology Dr. Robert E. Emery, Director, Center for Children, Families, and the Law, University of Virginia, Charlottesville, Virginia

---

The Parenting Experts

There are many different experts to help you deal with child-related issues during and after your divorce. Many can be very helpful in developing the parenting plan, and many can give you strategies to help transition the children from one household to the other and back. There are professionals who can assist with dispute resolution when parenting issues are being debated, but who do not make decisions on custody and access issues; there are others whose decisions are binding. You can use these various professionals to help minimize parental conflict or improve cooperation. Many of these experts will try to develop your parenting skills so that professionals are not required on an ongoing basis.

There are many differences in the scope of expertise and authority of these specialists. What's more, the terms used for specific professionals vary by jurisdiction. Check with your lawyer to identify the appropriate professional to help you with your parenting issues and concerns.

Co-parenting Counselors

The role of a co-parenting counselor, also known as a parenting consultant, is to help parents develop the parenting plan, and to provide education and coaching on parenting issues during or after the divorce. This person does not act as a decision maker should there be a child-related dispute.

The co-parenting counselor often works with high-conflict families to clear up communication issues and parenting deficits and to help the co-parents set up goals and rules for their family. In these cases, the counselor will generally assist in setting up rules of conduct to ensure that everybody is treated well and with respect. He or she may also set up communication standards that include regular sharing of information and emergency contact conditions, and guidelines on how to pass along transition information. Parents usually agree to refrain from phone or physical contact and to engage in simple communications via e-mail only.

Co-parenting E-mail Rules

- Communication is to occur by e-mail only.
- The parties may initiate only one e-mail per day, and it must pertain to only one issue.
- If a response is not received from the other party within twenty-four hours, the same e-mail must be sent again.
- No e-mail may exceed one hundred words in length.

- The content of all e-mails must follow the rules of common sense and courtesy. No harsh tone. No rude behavior.
- If a child complains about one parent's behavior, the other parent should make no assumptions or complaints of his or her own without first sending that parent a courteous inquiry seeking explanation.
- If one parent makes an inquiry regarding the other's parental behavior, the latter should return a responsive message. "Responsive" means validating the other parent's concern and asking for more details about the alleged incident, apologizing for the mistake, providing a compromise solution, or scheduling a co-parent counseling appointment.

The reason a parenting expert is helpful to the family is because each spouse's lawyer is focusing only on the party that has hired him or her, so in most cases the kids really don't have a legal professional looking out for them.

The co-parent counselor works with each parent and the children separately to correct any parenting deficits and communication deficits. All of the data obtained during these meetings remains privileged, as agreed to in advance by the parents and their lawyers. Thus, the co-parent counselor's therapeutic alliance with each of the parents and with the children is protected. Neither party is able to use that professional's impressions or notes from the sessions in later legal actions. The data that are gathered during the individual parent sessions or during sessions with the parent and the children remain guarded so that posturing of the parents is reduced and the real work of creating healthier relationships can occur.

The parents work within the e-mail rules and do not engage in any further vocal or physical contact with each other. The co-parent counselor is copied on each e-mail and can intervene when necessary. If the co-parent counselor cannot counsel the parents to an agreement and declares an impasse, the e-mail record can be used for an arbitration conducted by a separate professional. An arbitration can occur within a very brief period of time, unlike returning to court. Very rarely will parents arbitrate during co-parent counseling. Nevertheless, if no decision can be counseled, the parents and children can move forward quickly with arbitration rather than being mired in months of legal action. In addition, because an independent judgment about the facts is made by an arbitrator, the therapeutic alliance with the co-parent counselor is preserved.

Psychologist and lawyer Dr. G. Andrew H. Benjamin, University of Washington, Seattle, Washington

The counselor can also assist in resolving scheduling conflicts, and provide guidance on how to make decisions together and how to raise and resolve parenting concerns that one parent may have about the other's home.

Parenting Coordinators

The parenting coordinator's role is to assist with the implementation of a parenting plan that has already been agreed to by the parties or ordered by the court. The coordinator has blended responsibilities; he or she provides parenting consultation and coaching, but also monitors the fulfillment of the parenting plan and has a limited amount of power to modify the agreement. This person may help the former spouses come to an agreement on disputed parenting issues, and he or she may make legally binding decisions of his or her own. The ultimate goal of parenting coordination is to protect and maintain safe, healthy, and meaningful parent-child relationships after a divorce.

What Is Parenting Coordination?

Parenting coordination is a form of alternative dispute resolution. It's used by the minority of families who remain entrenched in chronic conflict three, four, or more years after a separation or divorce, and for whom adequate assistance has not been provided by the courts. Although allowing one parent to make all final decisions may be necessary for some high-conflict families, it is rarely a sufficient strategy, as these families usually sweat the small stuff (after-school activities, temporary changes to access schedules for special events, the transfer of clothing and belongings, and so on) more than they do the major legal custody issues, such as educational or medical decisions. These high-conflict families struggle with implementing their parenting plan and argue incessantly about day-to-day matters.

Psychologist Dr. Barbara Jo Fidler, Toronto, Ontario

Depending on the jurisdiction, a parenting coordinator may also be known as a "special master," "wiseperson," "on-going ad litem," "parenting referee," "family court adviser," or "case manager." When selecting a parenting coordinator, it is advisable to choose an individual whose expertise is mental health, such as a psychologist, psychiatrist, or social worker, rather than a lawyer, whose expertise is the law.

Parenting Mediators

Just as you might call on a mediator to resolve financial disagreements, you can also use a parenting mediator to help you and your former partner reach an agreement regarding parenting issues. Unlike arbitration, mediation is a voluntary process, and the mediator acts as a neutral facilitator. The final decision still rests with you and your ex.

As in the case of a parenting coordinator, if you are using a parenting mediator to settle a child-related dispute, it would be preferable to select a mental health professional rather than a legal expert.

Arbitrators

Arbitration is a coercive process that can be mandated by the separation agreement should the parties have difficulty agreeing on parenting issues postdivorce. An arbitrator makes the decisions for you. One was involved in resolving some of my parenting issues. I felt extremely frustrated and intruded upon because a stranger was making decisions on behalf of my family. I felt that I knew my children better than the professional who made the decisions, and that the money I spent on arbitration could have been put toward benefiting my children instead.

That is difficult, to have a third party make your decisions for you, but it is even worse from the decision maker's perspective to see a couple who can't make fundamental decisions. Things most people would do without even thinking about, this couple struggles over, agonizes over, beats each other over—and they get nowhere.

Psychologist Dr. Michael J. Spierer, Madison, Wisconsin

Co-parenting After Divorce

When former couples finally reach a divorce resolution, whether through the courts or ADR, they might be thinking, "OK, now I can live happily ever after." It doesn't always happen that way. The parenting plan can be difficult to implement, and adjustments might need to be made along the way. Sometimes it can take a very long time to settle down and see what the new family structure looks like.

Co-parenting means that both you and your former spouse must take responsibility for raising your children, even though you are no longer husband and wife. The goal is to keep children out of the middle of your conflict so they don't feel the stress of the situation. The children should feel as though they still have a family, just one that has been reorganized. Of course, the ideal way to achieve this is for the parents to get along, do what is in the children's best interests, and put their children's needs before their own. I understand firsthand that sometimes this is easier said than done. If parents need help to reach these goals, then a parenting expert can step in.

Divorce is the dissolution of the legal contract between a married couple. It means the transforming of a family, not the ending of a family. When parents separate, it is better to think of the family as reorganized instead of broken. Everyone still needs each other. How parents handle the changes that occur because of the reorganization will have a direct effect on how well the children and parents fare after the separation. While change is often difficult, it doesn't have to be destructive. It makes sense to get psychological support during such trying times. There are a lot of mistakes that don't have to happen if parents are informed of the best way to solve their issues.

Dr. Jayne A. Major, Breakthrough Parenting
Services, Inc., Los Angeles, California

I have heard co-parenting stories that range from one extreme to the other. There are children who move effortlessly between households, and there are children who move back and forth with much conflict and angst. There are parents who cooperate extensively, who essentially raise their children together even while living apart, and there are parents who engage in *parallel parenting*, each raising the children on his or her own, with little contact with the other parent.

In my own co-parenting experience, I've found there are times when I am inconvenienced, when I have to be flexible with my schedule so that I can adapt to theirs. I'm not perfect. There are times when I've messed up and showed frustration and anger. But when I see my children's reaction, I realize that I was wrong, apologize to my children for my behavior, and try not to repeat it.

A parent's job is to help his or her children become emotionally healthy, caring, mature adults with a strong sense of self-esteem and confidence who can contribute effectively to society. Parents are their children's role models. Children are watching their parents closely for behavioral cues.

One thing that all of the therapists I spoke with cautioned me about is not to *parentify* your children. This is the clinical term for children taking on the adult role. You don't want your children to feel responsible for taking care of you or to take on the role of a friend. These behaviors take away their childhood. The message that needs to be communicated—not just verbally, but also by your actions as co-parents—is this: It's your job to be a child. You are not to take care of us. We will take care of you.

Co-parenting Goals and Considerations

The goals of two adults attempting to co-parent should be to effectively communicate with one another, to make decisions that are in the best interests of the children, and to accommodate the children's changing needs and schedules.

If your ex is your co-parent, then in all likelihood he or she is not leaving your life. You will continue to be involved with that person to some extent, and you will continue to be confronted by the characters and qualities of your ex that you have grown to resent. Oftentimes the dynamics of the marriage continue to play out after the divorce, and the focus on the children gets lost.

Co-parenting with your former spouse can become even more challenging when you have philosophical differences in areas such as education, tutoring, music, sports, dietary needs, and so forth. The list may be extensive, and what's important to you may not be as important to the other parent. Difficulties also arise when a parent puts his or her time with the children before the children's own needs.

Battling it out over such issues will never really achieve your objectives; it will just cost you more stress and money. The goal is not to punish the other parent; the goal is to let the children have the best lives possible.

There are not a lot of models for the nontraditional family. You have to get people to become creative with that sort of thing. If you look at the needs of the children, that's an easier process. But very often, you have an ex-spouse that doesn't want to cooperate. You have to remind that person, "This isn't about you; this is about your children. This is about them having good lives. This is about them maintaining a relationship with you as a parent."

Psychologist Dr. Michael J. Spierer, Madison, Wisconsin

You want to consider what the loss will mean if you sabotage a relationship with your former spouse or, unintentionally, with your children. You don't want to miss out on key milestones in your child's development because of how you handled a difficult divorce. You want to be involved throughout all of your child's milestones, from learning to ride a bike to learning to drive a car. You want to attend dance recitals and hockey games, to be involved with the many small things, from doing homework to carpooling.

Co-parenting Tips

- Stop and think about your children's needs rather than your own needs and preferences.
- Take time before you say things or make decisions that you will later regret because of the feelings you have toward your former spouse.
- Never say or put in writing anything that you would not want your children to read when they are grown up.
- Allow your children to participate in activities chosen by them, regardless of custody and visitation issues.
- Allow your children to freely take toys, clothes, and "transition objects" (such as iPods and laptops) between parents' homes.

Psychologist Dr. Philip M. Stahl, Gilbert, Arizona

Residence Issues

If divorced parents have children who move back and forth between two homes, they typically want those children to feel that each home is theirs. If your home is not the primary residence, you can still make your children feel special and comfortable, and not as if they are a visitor. A friend of mine who was not the primary parent once said to me, "I want my children to see my home as their home, not just a house they visit every other week. They have a closet to hang their clothes in and drawers to put them away in. They can leave anything they want or take what they want. But this is their home, too, not a vacation property."

If your children are old enough to understand, you might want to tell them: "We would both love to have you live with us all of the time. Both of us would like that. We want to make this work so that we can be with you as much as we can, yet let you be with your other parent, too. We both want to spend time with you."

Moving Between Mom's Home and Dad's Home

Transitioning between homes can be a stressful time for children. The easier a parent can make it, the better it is for them. Transition can also be difficult for you as a parent, because you're giving up your children for a period of time. But you must realize that this is not about you; it is about your children.

I remember that for the first few months when my children left to be with their father, they were not themselves when they came home. They were hyper and wound up. They would run to their bedrooms to make sure everything was still the same. It was a mixed bag of emotions for all. It's like they had one personality at their dad's house and another at mine. I was told that's normal. Children behave differently in different circumstances— they respond differently to friends than they do to teachers, for instance. Although I was aware of these differences, having them react differently to me certainly hit me hard.

I've learned to give my children their "adjustment time." I realized that they were sort of compartmentalizing their surroundings—from Mom's house to Dad's house. We now have a routine when they come home from their dad's. I usually make a little treat, they relax a bit, and then we snuggle and watch TV. Here are some other tips for easing the transition:

- Give children something to look forward to when they come home. Talk to them about what this could be—a special snack, alone time, a TV show to watch, and so forth.
- Involve your children in what they need to do when they come home (check e-mail, read, do homework—whatever offers them comfort and makes them feel at home).
- Ask your children: what can I do for you to make it easier for you?

Whether or not you like your former spouse and whether or not you agree with his or her parenting style, there is not much you can do about what occurs at the other home. Children are entitled to spend time with both parents. Your task is to send them off in the same way you would if you were sending them anywhere else where you wanted them to have a good time while they're away from you, such as camp or school.

This situation is more difficult, however. If your child were going to, say, a sleepover at a friend's, you could simply ask what time they went to sleep, what they ate and when, who else was over, and all of the other questions you might naturally want to know the answers to. But when your child is visiting the other parent's home, you may feel like the right to know what is going on has somehow been taken away.

One of the awkward things I had to get used to was the feeling that my children had another life that I had no involvement in nor any awareness of. Many times over the years I have been somewhere and met someone new, only to discover—much to my surprise—that he or she already knew my children. I found that I had lost touch in a sense; I had no way of knowing what my children were doing socially. I became absent from a part of my children's life, and that would not have happened had I not been separated.

When my children were younger, I didn't always know about their new friends and their friends' families. It wasn't an issue of control for me as much as it was about being in the know. As my children get older there are other concerns. It *is* a control issue now, in some sense—I want to know what environments my children are exposed to, because I might want to provide them with some kind of guidance. Again, being absent from a part of their life experiences is not always easy.

Parents must take their cues from their kids. Children whose parents have been in a lot of conflict or who have litigated over custody most likely will resist having conversations and answering specific questions about what they did at the other parent's house. These children have learned that the words they say in an innocent manner are sometimes used as weapons in a custody battle or fuel arguments between parents. So they learn to keep quiet, because they are afraid that anything they say may be used in some way they cannot anticipate.

Transition Tips on Discussing the Weekend

- Ask your children how their weekend was. To not ask about what goes on when they are apart from you would send the wrong message. Your child might think that you are just not interested, or that you can't stand to hear about them enjoying time with the other parent.

- The motivation for asking about the weekend should be to serve the child's needs, not to have your curiosity satisfied.
- When children sense that they are being used as spies to report on what is going on in the other home, or when you react to the news with frowns, raised eyebrows, or sarcastic comments, the kids sense that you are not genuinely interested in sharing their lives with them as much as you are about getting some gossip about the other family.

Psychologist Dr. Richard A. Warshak, Dallas, Texas

What If a Child Doesn't Want to Go to a Parent's Home?

Visitation refusal is a very serious issue. You must ask yourself, why is this happening? Could you or the other parent be doing something to destroy the relationship? Is it because of friction between your child and your or your ex's current partner? Are you not letting go when your child asserts a need for independence? There are so many variables to consider and discuss. Talk to your child to find the answer. If it is too difficult, perhaps you can talk it over with a parenting expert to see what can be done to avoid damage (or repair damage that's already occurred) to the relationship.

The most heinous situation in child custody disputes is called *pathological alienation* or *parent alienation syndrome* (PAS). In this scenario, one parent becomes obsessed with destroying a child's relationship with the other parent when there is no good reason to do so. Alienation can be mild, moderate, or severe. A parent is engaging in parent alienation anytime children hear him or her speak in a negative way about the other parent. In extreme situations, children are turned against a healthy parent. The children's will and choice are removed from them through a form of brainwashing. This is a serious form of child abuse, because if it isn't stopped, the children are headed for psychiatric disturbances, failed relationships, and dysfunctional lives in which they will pass this behavior on to their own children. If you suspect that your children are being deliberately alienated from you, consult the "Resources" section (page 188); both Dr. Richard A. Warshak and Dr. Jayne Major have researched the topic of parent alienation extensively.

Communication Issues

Communication Between Parent and Child

There are no specific rules on how to maintain contact with the children when they are with the other parent. It depends on the age of the child, the relationship the child has with the parent, the individual characteristics of the child, and the relationship the parents have with each other. Some children want a phone call and enjoy speaking to the other parent. Other children are not verbally expressive, which makes phone conversations frustrating and hard. It's interesting—my daughter calls me all the time, yet my younger son really does not like to be on the phone. I get one-word answers. Such responses can cause distress for the parent making the call, but I know that it is not a reflection of how he's feeling about being at his dad's house; that's just his communication style.

Phone Rules

- There should be an effort by both parents to allow contact between the child and the other parent, especially if that's what the child genuinely wants and the calls are helpful to the child.
- The younger the child, the more the contact is preferred.
- When a parent calls to speak to his or her children, have the children take responsibility for answering the phone or returning the call; giving a child the option of taking or refusing the call shows a lack of respect for the other parent.

- Do not use the phone to intrude on the child's time with the other parent or to maintain influence over the child when the child is in the other home.
- Do not use the phone to have the children spy on the other parent and report all the "bad things" that are going on.
- Use the phone in a way that serves the child's needs, not the parent's need to continue to influence the child and to interfere with the child's relaxation and enjoyment of time in the other parent's house.

Psychologist Dr. Richard A. Warshak, Dallas, Texas

Communication Between Co-parents

To reduce conflict, you and your ex-spouse must find a communication style that works for you. Do not use your children as messengers; it only worsens a deteriorating situation. Rely on e-mail, short conversations, whatever you need to do—just do not involve the children by making them act as the mouthpiece. Also, treat the other parent with respect. If you know you are going to bring the children home late, common sense would dictate that you call the other parent to tell him or her—something so simple, yet often overlooked.

Finding a way to put your children foremost in your mind is an effective strategy to avoid being drawn into marital battle. When you anticipate a difficult phone conversation with your ex, put a picture of your child in front of the phone to remind yourself for whom you're having the unpleasant conversation. Before beginning the conversation, clarify for yourself the one or two issues you plan to discuss. Do not let yourself get drawn into talking about other matters. This strategy helps prevent the free-for-all that often ensues when you call to discuss the need for a time change and end up screaming at each other over homework not done, teeth not brushed, and whatever else is bothering both of you that day. Be clear about what the issue is that you are discussing, and stick only to that issue.

Social Worker Elinor Gertner, Jewish Family and Child Service, Toronto,
Ontario

The Reconfigured Family

Creating structure within a co-parenting arrangement can be an exhausting balancing act. I am always juggling my children's schedules; my personal schedule; household chores; the children's activities, lessons, and appointments; and everything else single-handedly.

I found that each child has his or her own needs and reacts differently to the same situations. I made a point, especially when my kids were younger, to spend time alone with each of them; we called this occasion our "Mommy day," and it was a great bonding time. I would make arrangements for the other children to have a play date, and the two of us would do something special together—a movie, a bike ride, shopping, lunch—whatever he or she was in the mood for. Now that my kids are older, they are so busy with their own schedules that when one of them is home, I try to take advantage of that time to spend together.

Many divorced parents are saddened because they don't have the opportunity to see their children every day. While you do need to develop coping strategies, you have other opportunities to see your children outside of the parenting schedule. If your children are participating in an event such as a sports game, a dance recital, or something else that is in a public venue, and the event is not on your time, you can still attend. You will have to be responsible for your own ticket, but it sends a positive message to your children that you care about them all the time, not just when they are at your home.

Develop structure around your children and just be a good role model. It will help them adjust to the new family dynamic. Involving the children in the changes is also helpful for them. If they are going to be moving or getting a new bedroom, let them see the new home or pick out their new furniture. This will provide them with a sense of comfort in their new surroundings.

At the beginning of my separation, I started to develop new and different traditions that became part of our family restructuring. For instance, birthdays and special occasions were celebrated with a special ice cream cake that I wouldn't normally have bought. As my children get older, we continue to develop other routines and events to prevent everyone from running off in their own direction without any family time; dinnertime is an example of this. Everyone seems to get so caught up in their own activities that the traditional dinner sometimes becomes a chore. Of course, the truth is that these are activities that many families have trouble enjoying together, no matter how many parents are living at home.

You have to reconstitute a new family unit. In some ways, this can allow each of the parents to experience the kids in a different way, and the kids to experience the parents in a different way. Often the parental functions had been doled out to each parent, and now you have each of the parents having to do everything, really, and to meet the kids' needs and be responsive to the kids' cues in all areas. In some ways it makes the kids' relationships with each of the parents much richer. There is pretty good evidence to suggest that the prior level of involvement of a parent is not a particularly good predictor of the relationship that develops between that parent and the children post-separation. Divorce does afford an opportunity for each of the parents to be more meaningfully involved with the kids. It's often an eye-opening experience for each of the parents, and many times the relationships do deepen.

Psychologist Bruce Copeland, Bethesda, Maryland

Coping with the Born-Again Parent

Divorce can sometimes be a bit of an awakening for a parent and result in him or her actually becoming a better parent and taking a more active role in the children's lives. If you were the main caregiver before divorce and did most of the work, wondering why your ex couldn't take a greater parental role, his or her turnaround after the divorce can cause frustration and confusion. But while it may be upsetting at first, ultimately you should come to realize that it is better for your children to have both parents involved in their lives. It may also make things easier for you if you find that you can share responsibilities such as driving the children to their friends' homes, programs, and other events.

What I try to say to parents is this: "I know you really want that other parent to learn how to be a better parent. I know you're mad that he or she didn't step up to the plate before, but look at the good news. The good news is that now he or she is doing it, and this is great for the kids. Maybe it feels really unfair to you, and that's understandable. You have a right to be angry, but isn't this turnaround good for the children? Isn't this what you ultimately want?"

Psychologist Dr. Terri Romanoff-Newman, Minneapolis, Minnesota

Co-parenting When There Is Financial Disparity

Divorce can cause financial disparity. If you live in the home with the smaller budget, that doesn't mean that your children will love you any less. With a little creativity, you can still find many activities to keep the children involved—it doesn't always have to be about material things. Take your children to the park, for a walk, or on a bike ride. Community centers, park districts, and libraries offer programs that are often free or of minimal cost. Museums and other cultural institutions also have programs for children that are not always expensive. During the warmer months, free or low-cost street festivals can be a lot of fun.

If you are the wealthier parent, don't try to buy your children's love. It will cause them to become overly indulged and develop unrealistic expectations as they become adults.

Co-parenting When Your Ex Is in a New Relationship

Adapting to the idea that your former spouse is in a new relationship when you are not can be emotional. One attitude I have run across is, "Good. That person is no good, so my ex got what he or she deserved." That view is harmless if there are no children involved. But if you do have kids, let me ask you this: if the new partner really is no good, is that good for your children? Quite frankly, no, because you can't stop your children from being exposed to that person when they are with the other parent.

As much as it may hurt and feel awkward, you really should hope that your children like your ex's new love. If you know the new person is in fact a good person, you might want to tell your children that it is all right to like that person, so that your children don't feel like they have a loyalty issue.

What I suggest is that if you are dating somebody really significant, the other parent should get to meet that individual. It's not easy, but it's realistic. And if your ex can get through it, he or she can really feel good about his or her ability to handle things. You want your children to like the other person, because if they don't, then it's not in the children's best interests.

Psychologist Dr. Terri Romanoff-Newman, Minneapolis, Minnesota

And if your ex is a not a good role model, then maybe his or her new partner will be a good influence, which could only be good for your children.

In some cases, the former spouse's new partner can have a very positive influence, because he or she doesn't want the conflict to continue and is not interested in usurping a parental role. This can have a calming effect on the post-separation situation. In other circumstances, new partners just fan the fire, really cheer on their new spouse, and want control or want to be overly involved with the children. Many people enter a new relationship and inherit a second family, which is an important aspect of the culture that we live in. You're not just dealing with a former spouse; you're dealing with that person's new spouse, and his or her children, and how those children mix with your children.

Lawyer Nicole Tellier, Nicole Tellier Law Offices, Toronto, Ontario

The advice that therapists provide to stepparents or new partners is that they need to put themselves in the role of a friend, not a parent. Furthermore, this new partner should not be invested in the significant other's anger and resentment toward the ex-spouse. Stepparents and new partners need to be buffers against the conflict that the parents are having; they need to be the reality check.

New relationships can be skewed by the anger, sadness, despair of the recently divorced person and the picture that has been painted of his or her ex. So if Dad has a new relationship during a time when he's enormously unhappy with Mom, the girlfriend aligns herself with Dad and sees Mom through his angry eyes. And then what happens in co-parenting is that the Mom-and-Dad relationship improves and gets realigned, and they go back to somehow finding a way to be friendly with each other. And so now they've made a shift, but the girlfriend is still holding on to all that anger.

Psychiatrist Gary Chase, Santa Monica, California

Co-parenting as Your Children Mature

Children's needs change. How can you anticipate what high school your child should attend when he or she is just entering nursery school? Or think about overnight camp when your child isn't even sleeping through the night yet? What is appropriate at age two might not work when your child is twelve. As children grow, their needs change, and this needs to be accommodated. As your children get older, a parenting plan that was developed when they were very young needs to be revisited. Some parents find it hard to change the parenting schedule, especially if it feels as though they are losing time with the children. But flexibility and change are vital to effective co-parenting.

What you need to do is move away from the concept of "losing time" and move toward maintaining a positive, strong relationship with your children. Parents are often so focused on the first eighteen years of the child's life. What they are really doing during that time is setting the groundwork for the longer-term relationship with the child, which is after they are eighteen. What you want to do is to establish communication, nurturing, and an interest in being together and sharing holidays, rituals, activities, and pursuits. Once the children are off on their own, that relationship continues, and parents find themselves not only in a relationship with their children, but, theoretically, in a relationship with their grandchildren as well.

Psychologist and parenting consultant
Mindy Mitnick, Minneapolis, Minnesota

Flexibility is especially important as your children enter their teen years. Teenagers are self-centered. Teenagers are fickle. Teenagers tend to see their parents for what they can offer—a wallet (money), a fridge (food, food, and more food), a bed (a place to sleep all day) and a car (with you as either their personal chauffeur or the "giver of the car keys"). I noticed that as my children got older, they suddenly became embarrassed to hang out with me. But having spoken to other parents both married and single, I know that the challenges of teenagers are universal, regardless of their parents' marital status.

Don't mistake your teenager's struggle for independence, or his or her desire to spend more time with friends or on the Internet, for symptoms of your divorce. As children reach their early or mid-teens, their peer groups become essential to their lives. They don't care about Mom's time or Dad's time; they just care about their own time. Their whole life focuses around their friends, which is normal—their primary focus is on themselves. It's not a bad thing; it's just the way it is. My son often tells me, "I know it's your weekend, Mom, but this is a time that I need for myself; I need to work on a project with friends," or go to a party—or he has some other arrangement. A teenager who is basically healthy, who relates well to his or her parents, but who wants the freedom to make his or her own age-appropriate choices, is different from one who is caught up in taking sides in his or her parents' dispute.

Many parents also complain that their children never let them know ahead of time what they will be doing, but that may be because the children themselves do not really know; that's not how children make their plans. They get on their computers, they instant message each other, and the plan emerges, sometimes within a space of fifteen minutes. All of a sudden, they are busy and on their way to join up with friends.

Teenage behavior can be hard to take sometimes. One Saturday evening, both my older son and I were home. I said, "Let's go to a movie." He said no. I offered to pay, told him he wouldn't need to use his allowance, but still he refused. He went to his room, turned on his computer and proceeded to communicate with his friends. I went to him later and said, "You don't want to be seen with your mother—that's it, isn't it?" He blushed a bit and said yes under his breath. But that's a teenager, like it or not; it has nothing to do with divorce. (OK, he did agree to spend two evenings with me when I took him to Deep Purple and Queen concerts. Even though my ears rang for two days, it was worth it.)

The teen years can be especially hard for noncustodial parents. If you live an hour away from your child's primary residence, where his or her school and peer group are, that makes it tough for the teenager to really enjoy his or her time at your home. As difficult as it may be for the noncustodial parent, most times that parent needs to take a backseat role to the person who is the custodial parent.

Noncustodial parents have the fantasy that their kids are spending every minute in the other parent's home directly interacting with that parent, which is not true. As the children get older, the noncustodial parent needs to understand that, at that age, children are not going to be spending much one-on-one time with either parent if the relationship is going well. At the same time, I have sympathy for noncustodial parents, because they have missed out on the daily contact with the child that they expected when the child was first born. And, in a sense, they feel that they want to compensate. The mistake they make is thinking that the way to compensate is just by spending more time with the child, or by insisting on maintaining a schedule for a sixteen-year-old that was created when the child was six. Those parents need to find ways to connect with their children without interfering with the children's natural development. This can occur during vacations or summertime. If feasible, noncustodial parents should consider moving closer to the children in order to be part of the fabric of their lives instead of having long-distance relationships.

Psychologist Dr. Richard A. Warshak, Dallas, Texas

Some parents are adamant that their children spend time with them when it's "their time." They may even stop the children from participating in activities or programs or spending time with their friends. It is foolish to place your desire for contact with your child above promoting his or her healthy development. Try not to think in terms of minutes and hours; think in terms of the quality of the relationship you are building and sustaining.

You Can't Be Mother and Father

The dynamics of transforming the family can sometimes be hard. Sometimes a child is at a stage where he or she requires more support from a father or a mother. When my son started to shave, he certainly didn't want me to teach him. And as my daughter started to mature, shopping for specific undergarments wasn't something she looked forward to doing with her father.

A lot of girls get uncomfortable with their dads when they get into their preteen years, and they balk at visiting as often as they did or as long as they did. But dads have an awful lot to offer teenage girls in the way of guidance, morals, and other things like that.

Marriage and family therapist Renee Leff, JD, Board Certified
Diplomate Fellow in Forensic Science, Encino, California

Fear of Losing Your Child's Love

Most parents love their children unconditionally and unselfishly. After divorce, they often experience fear that they'll lose their children's love, jealousy that they have to share love, or anxiety that their children love the other parent more. There can be a sense of competition for the children's affections. Especially early on during the move into two separate households, insecurity can cause your imagination to run rampant. The perceived threat is intensified when the other parent is able to provide more than you can, does not discipline like you do, or tries to be more of a friend than a parent. How do you achieve a feeling of emotional security? It is very helpful to turn to your support system: friends, therapist, clergy, and support groups.

I remember arguing with one of my children one day about doing homework. I knew that the rules were different at their father's house. The response I got was astounding—quite insightful, actually—and may give you some peace of mind. My son said, "Mom, you know that I don't like to do my homework, and I know you have rules, but your pushing me also shows that you love me."

The big fear in shared custody arrangements is that the kids are going to opt out of the arrangement. Often the parents live in fear that the children are going to someday decide that they don't want to be spending as much time as they are with one of the parents. As a result, parents become afraid to parent. They unconsciously create an appealing environment for their kids—they don't want to challenge them too much, don't want to do too much of the heavy parenting—and the kids in these arrangements sometimes develop very large senses of entitlement. They become used to having so much focus placed on them in each of the households, and the parents set firm limits so infrequently, that the kids develop an expectation that things will always be focused on them and kind of go their way. That way of thinking doesn't prepare them very effectively for life and for how the rest of the world is going to be treating them.

Psychologist Dr. Bruce Copeland, Bethesda, Maryland

The worst thing is for children to feel torn. All therapists suggest that the message you need to give your children is that it is safe to love both parents, not that your child cannot love one parent because the other will be upset. Children who are forced to take sides will feel torn, lost, and angry. Children have to learn to evaluate each parent based on how he or she treats the child, not on what the parents think of each other.

Parenting Tips for Transforming Your Family

Make a family calendar and hang it wherever the children will see it, to show that you care. Make your children see that their lives are important to you and that they are your priority.

On the family calendar, list:

- birthdates
- school schedules
- other dates, such as dental appointments, dance recitals, sports games, and so on.

Establish rules such as the following:

- Each parent must order his or her own tickets for children's events.
- Each parent must make his or her own arrangements at school to get information.
- It is not up to your former spouse to do those things or provide information for you.
- It's up to you to take the initiative.
- Don't make your son or daughter into the man or woman of the house.
- Don't turn your son or daughter into your best friend and confidant.
- Don't fill the void in your bed by allowing your child to sleep there. If you eventually start a relationship and no longer allow your child into your bed because you are sharing it with someone else, the child could feel displaced.

If you are the noncustodial parent, here are some ideas to help you maintain a positive relationship with your children:

- Some schools allow children to leave the grounds for lunch; you may be able to take them out to lunch without affecting the custodial parent's time. (But note that you may need permission from the custodial parent to do so.)
- As much as you can, duplicate at your home the little things that your kids love at the custodial parent's home—things like special Barbie dolls, books, and so on. Send out the message that you care. Duplicating items will remove the stress children may feel about taking their favorite things to the other parent's home or about forgetting to bring them (but keep in mind that some items, like the favorite blanket or stuffed animal, can't be duplicated).

Here are some ideas on how to maintain connections with teenagers:

- Check in with your kids via their cell phones and e-mail accounts just to say, "What's up?"; "How was your day?"; and so forth. Checking in helps ensure that you have as much input with your kids as their friends do.

- Be flexible; be an open door. Invite kids over either after school or for a few hours on the weekend, or just to have dinner, rather than for the full evening or weekend. You can say, "You are welcome the entire weekend, but I won't be upset if you want to be with your friends; you tell me if it fits in. If not, and you want to be with your friends, I'll drive you." If you pressure your kids to give up time with their friends in order to be with you, it will only backfire, causing your children to avoid you.
- If there are big differences in ages between siblings, plan one-on-one time with each child.

Lawyer Avra Rosen, Law Offices of Avra Rosen, Toronto, Ontario

Adjusting to your new family creates all kinds of new opportunities and new challenges. You need to be focused and think ahead. What's next? In order to live happily ever after, you need to consider how you will develop a new life for you and your kids.

The people who don't have a clue are the ones who need to become focused on planning. You can't get proper instruction from them unless they have some goals in mind and unless they are looking forward. A lot of people, especially those who have no concept of what life is going to be like a week from now, let alone two years from now, need help in starting to plan, organize, and direct some of their time and effort toward their future life. I always use the analogy that it's like a car. The reason a rear-view mirror is so much smaller than a windshield is that you should be spending a lot less time looking back than looking forward.

Lawyer Jim Stoffman, Taylor McCaffrey, Winnipeg, Manitoba

9

Moving On

Life is like a book: some chapters are more difficult to get through than others. When I started living on my own again, I thought about how the new chapters of my own life were going to be written. I began to ask myself many questions. Can people actually be single and happy postdivorce? If they can, how do they achieve this? What is their secret? Is it like one of those new fad diets—just follow these few simple steps and, poof, a new you, easily transformed while you sleep? Or can you only reach that elusive goal of happiness when you find that perfect mate—your knight in shining armor or damsel in distress?

You need to manage the emotional agenda so you can look on divorce not as something that's dreadful, but as a passage that you can then learn from. There are learning curves involved in all passages. You need to ask yourself if you are willing to learn.

Psychologist Dr. Bruce Derman, Woodland Hills, California

Divorce is about helping two people find a way to separate, yet some people just separate without working anything out. I've known some wonderful people who, five or ten years after their divorce, were still bitter and angry, still asking, "Why me?" and, "How dare you?"

There are couples that, many years after their divorce, are still fighting over many different issues. They've really never gotten over the emotional divorce. They are still holding onto emotional agendas. They say, "You've hurt me more than I've hurt you. I feel I was the right one in our marriage, not you." And when you are stuck in an emotional agenda, there's no time limit. It can go forever.

Psychologist Dr. Bruce Derman, Woodland Hills, California

Who did this attitude help? They were stuck in their past and finding it hard to live in the present. They were still so emotionally scarred—still walking around feeling wounded and bruised, still grieving and venting to anyone that would listen, still complaining about how their ex cheated them out of a life together. I didn't want to end up like this, so what could I do to move on?

"Smart" refers to your head and how you are thinking about this. But a divorce that is not only smart but wise is one that also doesn't leave behind people's hearts, including broken hearts, as they go through this. A good mediation allows space for grieving so that at the end of this process, the couple has more than just a good settlement financially; they also have been able to have some closure on the ending of this marriage.

Mediator Dr. Carl D. Schneider, PhD, Mediation Matters, Bethesda, Maryland

Coping with Your Ex After Divorce

People have different emotions and experiences when disentangling from a former spouse. Some are saddened by the loss of the person with whom they had hoped to spend the rest of their life. Others are thrilled to finally be apart. Still others are required to maintain a relationship for the sake of the children. Some people never want to see or hear about their former partners ever again. Others try to keep tabs on them; they become competitive and curious about what the other is doing and who he or she is dating, and they can become saddened by seemingly being replaced so easily. Whatever the circumstances, this is new, uncharted territory that you need to explore in order to adjust and move forward.

Disentangling and Reframing

Disentangling from your ex is about reestablishing personal boundaries between yourself and that ex-partner in order to reduce the amount of emotional damage that each of you can do to the other.

The number-one coping strategy is to get yourself in a position of wanting very little from your ex-spouse. The less you want from your ex, the less frustrated you will be. You have to work hard at that. It takes a lot, sometimes, to get to that position.

Psychiatrist Dr. Gary Chase, Santa Monica, California

When parents divorce, they need to move from an intimate relationship to a business relationship. It's not the other parent's business who's sleeping with the ex-spouse or what the ex is doing with his or her life, unless that behavior detrimentally affects the children. Once the finances are settled, the only business ex-spouses should have with each other is in taking care of their mutual parenting responsibilities to the best of their abilities. Some parents become obsessed with knowing what the other parent is doing and become out of control. The purpose of divorce is to allow each person to move on with his or her life according to what makes sense to him or her. The goal is to solve problems instead of escalating them. The best policy is to take the high road and keep peace in the family by keeping the relationship businesslike.

Dr. Jayne A. Major, Breakthrough Parenting
Services, Inc., Los Angeles, California

Some people find this difficult; they become immobilized in an emotional vortex that pulls them deeper into despair. When this happens, therapists suggest looking at things from a different perspective—reframing—and realizing that if you couldn't change your spouse when you were married, you are certainly not going to change that person now. Even if you have legitimate reasons not to trust your former spouse, therapists say, even though you are feeling victimized, you need to arm yourself with the understanding that the only thing you can change is your own attitude—and that you *must* change it to keep yourself from going down a self-destructive path.

You need to figure out how you can manage the other parent—how you can respond to him or her and how to react and not react to get what you want. It's not about blaming the other parent. It's really about looking at the self. The more blaming and externalizing of the other parent, the less productive your whole experience will be for you and for your kids. You can blame, criticize, and be hysterical, or you can try to figure out a way to manage so that you get a positive outcome.

Psychologist Dr. Barbara Jo Fidler, Toronto, Ontario

Develop a New Divorce Story—the "Third Story"

You know how inquisitive everyone around a divorcing couple can be. Everyone wants to know, "What happened?" The implication is that someone must be at fault, which causes divorcing individuals to feel they have to defend themselves, even when there should be no defense. As a result, many people come up with their own "divorce story," which is all about blame.

Ten Reasons We Get Stuck in Conflict

1. Conflict defines us and gives our lives meaning. An enemy is a quick, easy source of identity, because we are whatever they are not. By defining our opponents as evil, we implicitly define ourselves as good.

2. Conflict gives us energy, even if it is only the energy of anger, fear, pain, jealousy, guilt, grief, and shame.

3. Conflict ennobles our misery and makes it appear that we have suffered for a worthwhile cause.

4. Conflict safeguards our personal space and encourages others to recognize our needs and respect our privacy. For many of us, conflict seems to be the only way of effectively declaring our rights, securing the respect of others, restoring our inner balance, and protecting ourselves from boundary violations.

5. Conflict creates intimacy, even if it is only the transient, negative intimacy of fear, rage, attachment, and loss.

6. Conflict camouflages our weaknesses and diverts attention from sensitive subjects we would rather avoid discussing.

7. Conflict powerfully communicates what we honestly feel, allowing us to vent and unload our emotions onto others.

8. Conflict gets results. It forces others—those who only seem to respond to our requests or do what we want when we yell at them—to heed us.

9. Conflict makes us feel righteous by encouraging us to believe we are opposing evil behaviors and rewarding those that are good.
10. Conflict prompts change, which feels better than impasse and stagnation.

Mediator and lawyer Kenneth Cloke,
Center for Dispute Resolution, Santa Monica, California

Kenneth Cloke, Lenard Marlow, and Carl Schneider, all mediators, explained the concept of letting go of "his story" and "her story" to arrive at the "third story" about the divorce. The idea is to help partners uncouple in a more amicable way by having each spouse do a little soul-searching about how he or she contributed to the problems that resulted in divorce, take some responsibility for the marriage breakdown, and let go of blame. This helps them create a new version of the story they are telling about their breakup—one that isn't about blame and rehashing the past, but instead leads them into the future, where they can release each other.

The way that you have organized the experience of your marriage, and now divorce, leads to one and only one possible conclusion. That is because implicit in every question is its answer. If you see what happened to you as a crime—and it will be difficult for you to see it any other way—then there must be someone who committed that crime. There must be someone at fault. . . .

What I am going to suggest, therefore, is not that you change your answers, but that you let go of your question. Your answers haven't helped you make any sense of what has happened to you. Like all crimes, and even more so of tragedies, what has happened doesn't make any sense. That is why we are left with such painful feelings.

Mediator and lawyer Lenard Marlow, Divorce Mediation Professionals, New
York, New York; from his book The Two Roads to Divorce (n.p.: Xlibris 2003)

Creating Your New Life

Embrace an Uncertain Future

Your job after divorce is to create a better life than the one you had before. Life is now a journey into the unknown. This may seem overwhelming, but try to look at it positively, because it can be very exciting.

I didn't realize when I separated that I had embarked on an adventure to some mysterious destination yet to be determined. But this much I can say for sure—I knew I had to do something when I realized that life would pass me by if I just waited for that perfect mate. Not growing, I would be a boring person who could summarize a full year's living in less than five minutes. So I opened myself up to many new experiences and opportunities, and along the way I have become a very different person.

The difficulty I now have is reconciling who I am today with who I was during and even before my marriage. I now have long, straight hair, when before I had short, curly hair. There are fine lines around my eyes. I've changed. The changes are more than just physical, however. I have had so much more life experience. Not only am I learning to settle into the new me, but my parents, brother, sister, and friends have had to adapt, too. They find it interesting to relate to this newly introspective, assertive, smart, sensitive, and, dare I say, sexy woman.

Life is certainly different as a single woman in my forties than it was when I was single in my twenties. I now have a sense of who I am. Responsibilities and worries that I never thought about are now a reality. I am much more mature, realistic, and comfortable with where I am in life. Therapy, my children, friends, and family helped me achieve this perspective. I consider myself to be very fortunate. Not only do I have three amazing children and an extremely supportive family, but also an incredible group of dynamic friends. I certainly did not have such a rich life when I separated. I gained it through a lot of hard work and a desire to be content and happy.

Develop a Stronger, Happier You

It's important for you to think of yourself not just as a newly single woman or man, or as a mother or father, but as someone who is so much more. A worker, a friend, a volunteer—there are so many roles that you can play. You need to weave these other roles into your definition of yourself.

Now is the time to evaluate what you would like your life to look like, and to develop strategies to get there. If you were the primary caregiver and stayed at home with your children during your marriage, perhaps you need to go to work but haven't been in the workforce for a number of years. You could consider going to a vocational coach to help you make the transition. Perhaps you can afford to continue not working, but will this still be fulfilling? You can volunteer or pursue other interests. After all, your children may no longer be with you every day or weekend. The challenge is to rebuild your life to achieve a new kind of happiness. You just have to want to change and believe that it can be accomplished.

Visualize your life being different, and live your life as you envision it. Don't wait to do the things that you promise yourself you will do when you feel better. Start doing those things now, and happiness will follow. If you wait until you are happier to do those things, you will be waiting a long time.

I don't want to sugarcoat things. There are times when life post-divorce is difficult, sad, and lonely. You might still be experiencing a sense of loss, a setback in terms of self-esteem, or shame at no longer being part of a couple. But there are many single people living very rewarding lives. Again, try to reframe the situation and reflect on the life you actually had when you were married. I have heard people say that although they may have been blindsided by their divorce, when they really think about their marriage they realize that they were not fulfilled. If you are having difficulty postdivorce, this is when you really need to work hard to regain a positive outlook and work toward self-acceptance. Talking to a therapist, having a strong support network, or just asking yourself many questions about your life's goals can lead you to an evaluation of where you are headed and how to get there.

If you experienced physical or emotional abuse, then you were a victim. But your challenge now is not to live your life as a victim—to heal yourself, not blame yourself, and to find ways to move on.

There are various processes we can go through to help understand your current feelings, understand what your history has been about, understand where you came from. Through these processes and your interest in making some changes, we can explore what you can learn from these feelings and events, and where would you like to go with them.

Psychologist Dr. Joan Pinkus, Vancouver, British Columbia

Of course, moving forward does not happen overnight. People are sometimes in a rush to make it all better, but that is just masking reality. Therapists acknowledge that you need time to understand your feelings, help any children you have work through the divorce, balance life, and move positively toward the future. During this process you need to be good to yourself, cut yourself some slack, and make time for healthy habits. Recognize that how you feel now will not be how you feel a year, or two, or three years from now.

One of the things I suggest to people is that they work both internally and externally. Internally, meaning we have thoughts, we have feelings, we have actions. That sort of defines what we are. We think things, we feel things, and we do things. You don't want to spend too much time on any one of the three. When you realize that you're thinking too much, go out and do something—go to a movie, or whatever. Or if you're spending too much time doing—for instance, spending money that you don't have—stop and do some thinking and feeling.

Psychiatrist Dr. Mark Goulston, Los Angeles, California

Therapists also suggest that you focus on hope, and see divorce as an opportunity for personal growth. For instance, what will you do with the time you have when your children are not with you? How can you use that time productively?

The truth is that there was at least one other time in your life when you were single, and that there were good things about being single. It's helpful to focus on that, and to understand that there is an excellent chance— if you have a healthy relationship with yourself—that you are going to attract other people who have healthy relationships with themselves, and some of those people might potentially be good partners. If you can work on being at peace with yourself—if you wake up and you can say as a single person, "I'm going to have a good day. I'm committed to making that happen,"—I think that you could be at peace. And if you do find a partner to share that with at some point in time, all the better. But that's the frosting on the cake.

Psychologist Dr. Dan Baker, Director, Life Enhancement
Program at Canyon Ranch, Tucson, Arizona

Dating, Relationships, and Fun

Dating after marriage is certainly not the experience it was before marriage. Some people are able to jump into a new relationship right away, and others are more cautious. Sometimes people suddenly exhibit very adolescent behavior where dating is concerned; just recognize that it is a phase.

Many people have told me that they did not share much intimacy with their spouses toward the end of their marriages—not just physical intimacy, but the emotional part, too. Their egos and self-esteem had reached an all-time low moving through divorce. In a sense, newly single people, both men and women, are looking to prove to themselves that someone can be attracted to them and that they can have healthy adult relationships; as a result, they are just not ready for a serious committed relationship.

Be careful not to confuse feelings of lust, or the desire to be in love, for love. It's all right to go out and date and be with Mr. or Ms. Right Now as opposed to Mr. or Ms. Right; just make sure you understand that that's what you're doing. You may get into a relationship prematurely, and not really be ready for it, but that is all part of the learning process.

Falling in love is a very interesting phenomenon. What happens is that people see the world differently; they really do see it through rose-colored glasses. Falling in love produces a very erotic and sexual state of being. When you begin to fall out of love, you wake up one morning, see your partner, and suddenly realize that he's two inches shorter than you'd thought; that she has scars you've never seen; that he is twenty pounds heavier than you'd imagined, and so forth. And then you come to that proverbial fork in the road as to whether or not you are going to learn to love this person. And that's a very different proposition. You've heard people say, probably millions of times, "Well, I love him, but I'm not *in* love with him." "I love her, but I'm not *in* love." But the thing is, they're looking for that high to fill the hole in their own soul.

Psychologist Dr. Dan Baker, Director, Life Enhancement Program at Canyon Ranch, Tucson, Arizona

---

Divorced people sometimes feel that they have lost a certain skill set—that of communicating, flirting, and feeling comfortable just being with the opposite sex. You probably will have fears and anxieties about getting out there again. You must gather your confidence and just get out there. Meet people, have coffee—whatever you need to do to get that confidence back. Not every date has to end in a relationship. You might meet someone and really enjoy his or her company, but feel no chemistry between the two of you. That's fine; dates like this can still be fun, and maybe you will make a friend or two along the way. You can be philosophical about it: People come into our lives for many reasons. Is this someone you can learn from or have fun with? People lead to other people; you never know what kinds of connections you can make.

Be open-minded. You have had much more life experience since you met your former spouse, and your needs and desires might have changed since then. It is interesting how many people have said to me that they would never have given a certain person a second chance ten or twenty years ago, but now that they have had so much more experience and look at things differently, they are willing to explore someone's potential instead of measuring that person against the image of an ideal partner that they developed when they were much younger.

One of the wisest things someone's said to me is, "I'd rather be not married than to go through another one of these things again"—another divorce. So this woman made a list of all the attributes that a guy she would want to spend her life with would have. She wanted to keep them at the top of her mind so that if she ran into someone who had these qualities, she'd say, "Boy, this person has these things." But what she did next was really brilliant: she made a list of what that guy would be looking for in a woman. As she said, "It wouldn't be that great if I found the perfect catch, and I turned out to be a lemon." So she wrote down all the qualities he'd be looking for, then did a candid inventory of herself to determine where she needed to improve. She made a commitment to herself to overcome those things, because she wanted to become a good catch. And when she did start overcoming them, she started feeling more self-esteem, and she started attracting people.

Psychiatrist Dr. Mark Goulston, Los Angeles, California

New Relationships and Children

It's been said that dating is something that is good for you but can be hard on your children, because it pulls you away from them and may be confusing for them. There are no specific rules for dating when you have kids; there's no right or wrong way to do it. Of course, your priority should still be your children, and sometimes you have to sacrifice your needs for them.

You have to be careful how quickly you expose your children to the people you date. You can still go out and date, and have fun with friends, but your children (and even your friends) do not need to know your every move. Wait until you know that a new partner is someone special before you introduce him or her to the kids—but do introduce them to that person before he or she moves in or you get married again.

When the time comes for the introduction, you should discuss with your children that there is someone that you would like them to meet, rather than just springing it on them. Provide them with a sense of security that they are still your priority. If your children do not get along with your new partner, try to work it out. Don't ignore the situation in the hope that it will get better.

You might also want to introduce your new partner to the other parent. It's not so that they can be friends, but because this new person is now part of your children's world. Letting your ex meet your new partner gives your ex a sense of confidence as opposed to insecurity, and your children won't feel that they have the burden of a secret or that they can't talk about this new person with their other parent. And if your ex and your new partner actually like each other, isn't that better for the children?

Just Have Fun

I have found that just living my life and doing what interests me puts me in situations in which I can meet people. And if I don't meet someone on any particular occasion, well, at least I enjoyed what I was doing. I can't tell you the number of divorced people I have met over the years who couldn't bring themselves to go to a movie, take a walk, or just have a nice, quiet dinner by themselves on a Saturday night. They always had to be in a social environment, in the hope that they might meet someone. But oftentimes, they weren't enjoying what they were doing, met no one, and went home slightly depressed. Having a positive outlook is attractive to people, and those people will want to be in your company. If you come across as needy and desperate, this attitude will not win people over. Making friends and just having fun are also part of what makes for a smart divorce. Make time for yourself and enjoy what you're doing; it will lead to much more happiness and a more optimistic outlook.

You know, I find most people's perspective on divorce and how a divorced person should feel to be interesting. Many people have said to me, "Oh, you're divorced; I'm sorry." And my response has always been, "Don't be sorry; I'm happy." Living happily ever after—it's not just my experience. I know many others who have achieved the same goal.

Resources

Web Sites

Help Finding a Lawyer

American Academy of Matrimonial Lawyers

www.aaml.org

Members of the academy are highly skilled negotiators and litigators who represent clients in all areas of family law. These areas include divorce, annulment, prenuptial agreements, postnuptial agreements, marital settlement agreements, child custody and visitation, business valuations, property valuations and division, alimony, child support, and other family law issues.

Best Lawyers

www.bestlawyers.com

Here you'll find information on *The Best Lawyers in America*, a referral guide to the legal profession in both the United States and Canada. The Best Lawyers lists are compiled through an exhaustive peer-review survey in which thousands of the top lawyers confidentially evaluate their professional peers.

FindLaw

www.findlaw.com

FindLaw is designed to help you find information on specific areas of legal expertise. Topics may be browsed for the latest legal news, case law, and analytical articles relevant to a specific area of practice. An online resources section allows you to search for a case or research a lawyer.

International Academy of Matrimonial Lawyers

www.iaml.org

The International Academy of Matrimonial Lawyers is a worldwide association of practicing lawyers who are recognized by their peers as the most experienced and expert family law specialists in their respective countries. The academy Web site provides details on the members of the academy to the general public.

Lexpert

www.lexpert.ca/500/index.php

Lexpert offers one of the largest listings of professional lawyers in Canada. The lawyers listed have been recognized by their peers as leaders in their category of specialty.

Martindale-Hubbell

www.martindale.com

The Martindale-Hubbell legal network is currently powered by a database of over one million lawyers and law firms in 160 countries. Users can search by a variety of criteria, including name, geographic location, practice area, firm size, languages, and more. The network provides access to a wide range of biographical information and professional credentials of the lawyers on the site.

Help Finding Therapists and Other Divorce Experts

American Academy of Child and Adolescent Psychiatry

www.aacap.org

The American Academy of Child and Adolescent Psychiatry (AACAP) is the leading national professional medical association dedicated to treating and improving the quality of life of children, adolescents, and families affected by personality disorders.

American Board of Professional Psychology

www.abpp.org

The American Board of Professional Psychology (ABPP) serves the public and the profession by certifying that psychologists in various specialty areas of psychology have completed the educational, training, and experience requirements of that specialty, and that they maintain high ethical standards. You may visit the directory to search for a psychologist.

American Psychiatric Association

www.healthyminds.org/locateapsychiatrist.cfm
The American Psychiatric Association (APA) is a national medical specialty society whose physician members specialize in the diagnosis and treatment of mental and emotional disorders and substance abuse. To locate a psychiatrist in your area, contact the APA Answer Center. You will be directed to a local APA district branch, medical society, or mental health association that may be able to provide you with contact information for psychiatrists in your area.

Institute for Divorce Financial Analysts

www.institutedfa.com
The Institute for Divorce Financial Analysts (IDFA) is the national organization dedicated to the certification, education, and promotion of the use of financial professionals in the divorce arena.

Alternate Dispute Resolution Sites

Association of Family and Conciliation Courts

www.afccnet.org
The Association of Family and Conciliation Courts (AFCC) is an interdisciplinary and international association of professionals dedicated to the resolution of family conflict. The AFCC promotes a shared approach to serving the needs of children among those who work in and with family law systems, encouraging education, research, and innovation, and identifying best practices. The Web site provides resources for parents and professionals.

Family Mediation Canada

www.fmc.ca
Family Mediation Canada (FMC) is an interdisciplinary association of lawyers, social workers, and human services and health care profession-

als who work together to create a better way to provide for cooperative conflict resolution relating to separation and divorce, adoption, child welfare, wills and estates, and parent-teen counseling. Information and referrals to family mediators across Canada are provided.

International Academy of Collaborative Professionals
www.collaborativepractice.com
The International Academy of Collaborative Professionals (IACP) Web site provides a list of all collaborative practice groups in all countries where collaborative law is practiced.

Mediate.com
www.mediate.com
Mediate.com, "the world's dispute resolution channel," provides information about mediation, mediator selection, and the many areas in which mediation can be effective.

Helping Children and Families

Alliance for Children and Families
www.alliance1.org
The Alliance for Children and Families is a not-for-profit membership association representing child- and family-serving organizations in the United States and Canada. It works to support the professional staff of member agencies (including social service organizations and residential treatment facilities) who, in turn, assist the public.

Association of Jewish Families and Children's Agencies
www.ajfca.org
The Association of Jewish Family and Children's Agencies (AJFCA) is the membership organization of more than 145 Jewish Family and Children's Service agencies and specialized human service agencies throughout the United States and Canada. Member agencies provide preventive social services to children, adults, the elderly, and those with special needs in the Jewish and general community.

Child Welfare League of America
www.cwla.org
The Child Welfare League of America (CWLA) is a membership-based child welfare organization. It is committed to engaging people everywhere in promoting the well-being of children, youth, and their families, and in protecting every child from harm.

National Association of Christian Child and Family Agencies
www.naccfa.org
The National Association of Christian Child and Family Agencies (NACCFA) is a group of Christian agencies joined together in fellowship and mutual encouragement to address issues surrounding child and family care from a Christ-centered perspective.

Parenting Support and Education

Bonus Families
www.bonusfamilies.com
Bonus Families is the only international nonprofit organization dedicated to promoting peaceful interactions among divorced or separated parents and their combined families.

Breakthrough Parenting
www.breakthroughparentingservices.org
Run by Dr. Jayne Major, this site offers advice for parents going through divorce. The site also features articles to help parents experiencing parent alienation syndrome.

Emery on Divorce
www.emeryondivorce.com
Dr. Robert Emery provides information on parenting plans, the effects of divorce on children, the grieving process, and his twelve-year study on the effects of divorce mediation.

Parents Without Partners
www.parentswithoutpartners.org
Parents Without Partners is the largest international not-for-profit membership organization devoted to the welfare and interests of single par-

ents and their children. By offering a friendly, supportive environment and encouraging the exchange of parenting techniques, it provides them with an opportunity for personal growth, increased self-confidence, and greater sensitivity toward others.

Rainbows

www.rainbows.org

Rainbows is an international not-for-profit organization that fosters emotional healing among children grieving a loss from a life-altering crisis. Rainbows provides state-of-the-art intervention and prevention curricula for the child or adolescent who is experiencing a divorce, death, or other painful transition in the family.

Up to Parents

www.uptoparents.org

The Up to Parents Web site offers a collection of information and wisdom from many parents and children who have experienced divorce. It also offers practical guidance that the creators of the site have read and heard from thoughtful professionals who have labored to serve the interests of families and children.

Dr. Richard Warshak

www.richardwarshak.com

Dr. Richard A. Warshak provides tips and information on many topics related to divorce. His site offers regularly updated features, including "Alienation Busters," that give advice to parents whose children are alienated or are in danger of becoming alienated from them.

Child Support Guidelines

SupportGuidelines.com

www.supportguidelines.com

This site is a comprehensive resource for the interpretation and application of child support guidelines in the United States. It provides access to the text of the child support guidelines for all fifty states and the District of Columbia. Although it is designed primarily for lawyers, it contains useful links and information for the layperson as well.

Department of Justice Canada: Federal Child Support Guidelines
www.justice.gc.ca/en/ps/sup
This site provides information on the Federal Child Support Guidelines, the regulations for setting child support payments under Canada's federal Divorce Act.

Help for Victims of Domestic Violence

National Domestic Violence Hotline
www.ndvh.org
(800) 799-7233
The National Domestic Violence Hotline (NDVH) is a not-for-profit organization that provides crisis intervention, information, and referrals to victims of domestic violence, perpetrators, friends, and families. The hotline answers a variety of calls and is a resource for domestic violence advocates, government officials, law enforcement agencies, and the general public. NDVH serves as the only domestic violence hotline in the United States and has access to more than five thousand shelters and domestic violence programs across the United States, Puerto Rico, and the U.S. Virgin Islands.

Shelternet
www.shelternet.ca
Shelternet is a Canadian national not-for-profit charitable organization committed to working toward the prevention of violence against women and their children. Shelternet is dedicated to decreasing barriers faced by women accessing help online, and to increasing the technological capacities of shelters for abused women and their children. The site contains special sections on topics such as understanding abuse, finding shelter, and abuse and children.

To find help in your local area via the Internet, use a search engine such as Google (www.google.com) to look up phrases such as "assaulted women's hotline," "domestic violence," "family violence," "abusive situations," and "shelters" along with the name of your city or area.

Call 911 or your local police if you are in immediate danger.

Books

Aspatore Books. *Inside the Minds: Leading Divorce Lawyers; Industry Insiders on Successful Tactics for Achieving the Best Results for One's Client.* Boston: Aspatore Books, 2004.

Baker, Dan, PhD, and Cameron Stauth. *What Happy People Know: How the New Science of Happiness Can Change Your Life for the Better.* Reprint edition. New York: St. Martin's Griffin, 2004.

Benjamin, G. Andrew H., and Jackie K. Golan. *Family Evaluation in Custody Litigation: Reducing Risks of Ethical Infractions and Malpractice (Forensic Practice Guidebook).* Washington, DC: American Psychological Association, 2003.

Briles, Judith, PhD, Edwin Schilling III, and Carol Ann Wilson. *Dollars and Sense of Divorce.* Chicago: Dearborn Financial Publishing, 1998.

Cloke, Kenneth. *The Crossroads of Conflict: A Journey into the Heart of Dispute Resolution.* Calgary, Alberta, Canada: Janis Publications, 2006.

Eddy, William A. *Splitting: Protecting Yourself While Divorcing a Borderline or Narcissist.* Milwaukee, WI: Eggshells Press, 2004.

Emery, Robert E., PhD. *The Truth About Children and Divorce: Dealing with the Emotions So You and Your Children Can Thrive.* New York: Viking Adult, 2004.

Gould, J. W. *Conducting Scientifically Crafted Child Custody Evaluations.* Sarasota, FL: Professional Resource Press, 2006.

Gould, J. W., and D. A. Martindale. *The Art and Science of Child Custody Evaluations.* New York: Guilford Press; in press.

Goulston, Mark, MD, and Philip Goldberg. *Get Out of Your Own Way: Overcoming Self-Defeating Behavior.* Reissue edition. New York: Perigee Trade, 1996.

———. *The Six Secrets of a Lasting Relationship: How to Fall in Love Again . . . and Stay There.* New York: Putnam Adult, 2001.

Irving, Howard H., and Michael Benjamin. *Therapeutic Family Mediation: Helping Families Resolve Conflict.* Thousand Oaks, CA: Sage Publications, 2002.

Major, Jayne A. *Creating a Successful Parenting Plan: A Step-by-Step Guide for the Care of Children of Divided Families.* Santa Monica, CA: Living Media 2000, 1998.

Marlow, Lenard. *The Two Roads to Divorce.* N.p.: Xlibris, 2003.

Phillips, Stacy D. *Divorce: It's All About Control; How to Win the Emotional, Psychological and Legal Wars.* Santa Ana, CA: ExecuProv Press, 2005.

Stahl, Philip M., Ph.D. *Complex Issues in Child Custody Evaluations.* Thousand Oaks, CA: Sage Publications, 1999.

———. *Parenting After Divorce: A Guide to Resolving Conflicts and Meeting Your Children's Needs.* Atascadero, CA: Impact Publishers, 2000.

Tesler, Pauline H., and Peggy Thompson, PhD. *Collaborative Divorce: The Revolutionary New Way to Restructure Your Family, Resolve Legal Issues, and Move on with Your Life.* New York: Regan Books, 2006.

Warshak, Richard A., PhD. *Divorce Poison: Protecting the Parent-Child Bond from a Vindictive Ex.* Reprint edition. New York: Regan Books, 2003.

Webb, Stuart G., and Ronald D. Ousky. *The Collaborative Way to Divorce: The Revolutionary Method that Results in Less Stress, Lower Costs, and Happier Kids—Without Going to Court.* New York: Hudson Street Press, 2006.

Wilson, Carol Ann. *Survival Manual to Divorce: Your Guide to Financial Confidence and Prosperity.* Ellicott City, MD: Marketplace Books, 2005.

Wilson, Jeffery. *Wilson on Children and the Law.* 3rd ed. Toronto: Butterworths, 1994.

Glossary of Legal Terms

These terms are commonly used in family law cases and are presented here courtesy of the Carole Curtis Law Offices in Toronto, Ontario.

action: Legal term for a lawsuit; also known as an *application*.

affidavit: Sworn evidence in a written format; a written statement of facts, made under oath and signed before a commissioner for taking affidavits, a lawyer, or a notary public. An affidavit is sworn evidence, and it has the same force as oral evidence given in court.

agreement: A written document reflecting the parties' resolution of disputed matters. An agreement can be made regarding any specific issue or variety of issues.

alimony: Ongoing payments from one spouse to the other; also known as *support* (or, in Canada, *maintenance support*).

allegation: Statement of facts contained in a pleading or affidavit, setting out what the person intends to prove.

answer: The second document in a divorce case, in which the second spouse responds to the first spouse's application, and in which he or she must admit or deny the allegations made in the application for divorce.

appeal: The process by which a higher court reviews an order or judgment from a lower court and determines whether or not there was an error. The losing party starts an appeal by serving and filing a "notice of appeal" within a specified period after the order or judgment was made.

applicant: The party who initiates a divorce or other lawsuit.

application: See *action*.

application for divorce: The first court document in a divorce, in which one spouse requests relief from the other spouse and sets out the allegations upon which these claims are based. Known in some jurisdictions as a *petition for divorce.*

attorney of record: The lawyer who places his or her name and address on a court document and files it with the court on behalf of a particular party. In most cases, the attorney of record may be served with all future documents in the litigation. From that point on, the lawyer (or someone acting on his or her behalf) is obliged to attend at every court date unless and until he or she is removed as attorney of record, either by court order or at the client's written request. Those instructions must be served on the other parties and filed with the court. Known in Canada as a *solicitor of record.*

change of venue: A change of the location in which a case is to be tried or heard.

contempt of court: The intentional failure of a person who is obligated to obey a court order or judgment to comply with that order or judgment. Contempt of court is punishable by fine or imprisonment.

contested case: Any case in which the court must decide one or more issues that are not agreed to by the parties. Cases are considered contested until all issues have been agreed upon or decided by the court.

counterclaim: A request for relief made by the respondent in a divorce case, in answer to the claims made by his or her spouse in the application for divorce. Known in some jurisdictions as a *counterpetition.*

cross-examination in court: The questioning of a party or a witness by a lawyer other than that party's lawyer or the lawyer who called that witness. Anyone who gives evidence in court on behalf of one party may be cross-examined by the other party's lawyer. The scope of cross-examination is very broad, and a wide range of questions are permitted. Cross-examination may be used in an effort to discredit a witness—for instance, to demonstrate that the witness has changed his or her testimony.

cross-examination on affidavits: See *deposition.*

default order or default judgment: An order or judgment granted by the court without having heard the other side's case, because that side failed to submit papers within the time allowed or failed to appear at the hearing.

defended: A lawsuit is defended when the respondent files papers either disputing the claims made by the applicant or asking for relief of his or her own. When the lawsuit is defended, it is considered a *contested case*, and a trial or hearing could result.

deposition: The testimony of a witness (usually one of the spouses) taken outside the court, under oath, and set down in writing. Depositions are taken for the purpose of discovering the facts upon which a party's claim is based, obtaining financial information, or discovering the substance of a witness's testimony prior to trial. Also known as *examination for discovery* or *cross-examination on affidavits.*

direct examination: The initial questioning of a party or witness in court or in a deposition by the lawyer who called that person to the witness stand. Also known as *examination-in-chief.*

disclosure: The full and honest sharing of financial information between parties in a case, as required by law. The rules of the court set out procedures regarding the sharing of this information.

discretion of the court: The degree of choice available to a judge to interpret evidence and make a legally acceptable decision.

endorsement on the record: The brief summary of a judge's decision, noted on the court file.

evidence: Documents, testimony, or other material offered to the court to prove or disprove allegations made in the court documents or presented in court by witnesses.

examination for discovery: See *deposition.*

examination-in-chief: See *direct examination.*

ex parte motion: See *motion without notice.*

filing of documents: The placing of court documents into the court file that is opened for that lawsuit. Usually, filed documents must be accompanied by proof that they have been served on the opposing party.

final judgment: See *judgment.*

financial statement: A detailed statement, taken under oath and in writing, regarding the financial situation of the person signing the statement. The financial statement sets out income, expenses, assets, debts, and every other aspect of that person's financial situation.

hearing: Any court proceeding in which evidence is heard for the purpose of resolving disputed issues. Evidence may be presented orally, or in writing as affidavits.

interim decision: A decision that is meant to be short term or temporary—for example, interim support or interim custody—usually to last between the time the interim decision is made and the end of the case. Interim decisions can apply to brief time periods (a number of months) or, if the case takes a long time to be resolved, to as much as several years.

joint property: Property held in the names of two or more people.

judgment: The order of the court ending the case; also known as a *final judgment*.

jurisdiction: The power of the court to rule on issues relating to the divorcing parties, their children, or their property.

law clerk: See *paralegal*.

litigation: A general term used to describe a lawsuit or court case.

maintenance support: See *alimony*.

minutes of settlement: A document signed by both divorcing spouses (or, in some limited circumstances, their lawyers) that sets out the details of the settlement reached. It may be incorporated into a court order to facilitate its enforcement.

motion: A written application to the court requesting an interim decision. A motion is usually made after advance notice has been given to the other side. The evidence that accompanies a motion is provided in the form of affidavits. You may or may not need to be present when a motion is considered, depending on the court that is hearing the motion.

motion without notice: An application to the court for relief that is intentionally not served on the other party—if, for instance, one spouse is afraid of the other spouse and is requesting a restraining order. Also known as an *ex parte motion*.

notice of motion: A document that is served upon the opposing party, advising him or her of the date and place of the court appearance at which the motion will be heard by the court.

order: The court's ruling on a motion, which sets forth the parties' rights and responsibilities. The order is valid as soon as it is made by the judge. However, it is the responsibility of the lawyers to have the order typed and to arrange for it to be signed by a judge and sealed with the court seal. If the motion was contested, the draft order prepared by one spouse's lawyer has to be approved by the other spouse's lawyer before it can be sent to court. It may take several weeks before the signed, sealed order is available.

paralegal: A trained person who assists the lawyer in the conduct of your case. Usually paralegals perform work that does not need to be handled by the lawyer directly, but that would have to be done by the lawyer (at a much higher hourly fee) if the paralegal were not available. Paralegals may issue and file documents at the court offices. In some jurisdictions these functions may be performed by a *law clerk*.

party: A word used to describe the individuals whose rights and responsibilities are being decided in a family law case. The parties are almost always the spouses, but other people can also become parties, usually by court order (for example, grandparents).

petition for divorce: See *application for divorce*.

pleading: A general name given to court documents such as the *application for divorce*, *answer*, *counterclaim*, and *reply*. A pleading is a formal written request to the court for certain relief, or the written response to such a request.

privilege: The right of a party to make admissions to a lawyer, doctor, marriage counselor, and certain other professionals that are not later admissible in evidence. The privilege between lawyer and client belongs to the client; it is the client's right to maintain this privilege or, if desired, to waive it.

record: A brief of all documents in a case, which will be referred to during the hearing of motions, applications, trials, and appeals. The records are served on the other parties and filed with the court.

relief: Claims; whatever a party to a family law case asks the court to do (such as grant a divorce, award support, enforce a previous court order, divide property, prevent certain behavior, and so forth).

reply: The court document filed in answer to the allegations made in a counterclaim.

respondent: The party that defends a lawsuit brought by another party— for example, you would be the respondent in a divorce or family law case that was brought by your spouse.

rules of evidence: The rules that govern if and how oral or documentary evidence may be presented at court hearings or depositions.

service of documents: Most court documents must be given to the other party and filed with the court in order to be valid. This is called serving documents. In most lawsuits, the original document of the suit must be served to the other party in person. Usually a neutral person (a process server) serves the documents. In order for documents to be filed with the court, it is usually necessary to provide proof that they have been served on the other party, which can be done via affidavit. Once a lawyer is involved with the litigation and puts his or her name on the court file, it may be possible to serve the lawyer with the documents by mail instead of serving the opposing party in person. It is always within the discretion of a judge to order personal service of any specific document.

setoff: A debt or financial obligation of one former spouse that is deducted from the debt or financial obligation of the other. For example, if an ex-wife owes her ex-husband forty-three thousand dollars, and the ex-husband owes his ex-wife eighteen thousand dollars, the ex-husband's debt is considered a setoff against the ex-wife's, and the net result is that the ex-wife will pay the ex-husband twenty-five thousand dollars.

settlement: An agreement by which pending or contemplated litigation is resolved outside of court. The details are documented in the minutes of settlement.

solicitor of record: See *attorney of record*.

status quo: The existing state of things; the leaving of things as they are without modification or alteration. "Things" can be anything from access arrangements to property rights.

summons to witness: A document served upon a person who is not a party to the case that requires him or her to appear and give testimony at a court hearing, or at a deposition outside of court. A summons is normally accompanied by the payment of a witness fee set by local statute, as well as a mileage fee for transportation costs. Failure to comply with the summons could result in punishment by the court.

support: See *alimony*.

testimony: Statements under oath by a witness in a court hearing or at a deposition.

transcript: A typewritten, word-for-word record of proceedings taken by a court reporter during a court appearance or deposition.

trial: A formal court hearing to decide disputed issues raised by the pleadings.

variation: A request to the court to change a previous order or a judgment.

witness: A person who gives evidence in a case. The witness could be a party to the case or someone who is not a party.

Index